PRETEND NO ONE IS SINGING

Cover Art by Marian Toews

1

I'm in a hospital bed, wearing a giant hospital gown with some sort of sleeveless vest tied in front. The vest is too small. I feel claustrophobic in it. I ask the nurses if I can take it off and they complain in broken English "Nobody is ever small enough to fit into that vest, we thought for sure you were the one!" They seem so disappointed I agree to leave it on.

***

I found out today at the doctor's office, that I have liver cirrhosis. The doctor told me he wouldn't let me leave the building without my agreeing to sign in to emergency at the hospital. My boyfriend; Edward, drove me here, saw me settled in, then left to get my things from home. I'm not allowed to leave my bed. I'm lying here with an I.V. tube in my arm, attached to a see-through bag of something suspended from a metal pole. There's a commode beside my bed but I'm not allowed to get up to use it without a nurse to help me, I have no balance, I might fall down.

***

I'm being wheeled down the hall on a stretcher. We pass patients sitting on chairs along the walls and nurses bustling. Past the front desk where a few people are here visiting or checking in, into a brightly lit room where a doctor and some nurses are waiting for me. I compliment them on the cheeriness of the room. I'm afraid and nervous, so I'm all smiles, acting on my best behavior.

They put me under, and when I awake, they tell me they drained 2 1/2 liters of fluid from my belly. Quite a feat, since I barely weigh ninety pounds. They've put a catheter in me with a plastic bag attached outside my body. I'm shocked. They tell me I won't have it forever, but I don't believe them.

***

I've been here for about a week, Edward comes to see me every day. I was taken back yesterday to have my catheter exchanged for an inside one. They said it was necessary anyway because the first one wasn't put in properly. They warned me that in putting in the new one, they might accidentally cut something wrong and I might leak.

When they wheeled me out of the operating room, a doctor from my ward was in the hall, waiting for me. I recognized him as the kindly doctor I'd seen when I first came here. The doctor who'd operated on me was surprised, he hadn't expected the second doctor to be there. The second doctor insisted on wheeling me on my stretcher back to my bed, even though he was told that an orderly would do it. He acted overly jolly about the whole thing, like he was terribly embarrassed, but determined to go through with this, whatever it was.

The original doctor made noises like he thought the second doctor was nuts, exclaiming loudly when he reached out with a pair of scissors and cut the special new hospital socks I'd been given. "There!" he beamed "Now they'll fit you better!"

Later, the original doctor came to me with a new, identical pair of socks. "To replace the ones that doctor ruined." he told me gently.

***

The nurses tell me I can just pee while lying in bed, it will go into the catheter. So I do. Pee streams out of me onto the sheets. Also, sure enough, they accidentally cut something wrong and so I'm leaking from my side.

Nurses come in several times a day to inject me, and check the bags of fluid hanging from the pole beside my bed. I have a tube in my arm with four separate, brightly colored ends for inserting new tubes that are run up to the bags. I've been given a blood transfusion as well. I don't know why.

Every time the nurses have to change my pee soaked sheets, they complain to me "This is a poor hospital! We can't afford to do as much laundry as you're giving us!" as though it's my fault. They say the same when I ask for a heated blanket. "We can't turn up the heat." they remind me as they grudgingly hand me a lukewarm blanket "This is a poor hospital, we can't afford to turn up the heat."

They change the bandage on my leak. They put tensor socks on me because my ankles are grossly swollen, complaining when I push them down because they hurt. I'm beginning to feel strange. Like

7

everything is not quite real somehow. To make things worse, the catheter has started to come out. About six inches.

***

I keep coming down with new ailments. Every few days, one of the doctors comes in and informs me of the latest, and what they're trying to do to fix me. Apparently I have pneumonia now. I guess that's why I can't finish a sentence without running out of voice. I nod and smile as if I know what's going on. I'm a germ infested wreck. My health, bad as it was, has deteriorated since I came here. I have to find a way to get out.

I'm beginning to feel paranoid. The nurses, led by a tall blond who reminds me of 'Paris' from 'Gilmore Girls', keep gossiping in the hall outside my door, and in their little cafeteria room across the hall.

The gossip is mostly about me. They regale each other with stories about how bad my diarrhea has become and how many times I wet the bed. They laugh and sneer until one kind nurse suggests they all try to get to me faster when I call for help to the commode. They all agree. Yet every time, when I call for help, they walk right past my door with a smirk.

The problem is, I have to go every ten minutes. I don't seem to have any control over my bladder and bowels. I hold on desperately until I can't wait anymore, then slide carefully off my bed. I'm always attached by the intravenous tubes and so I have to avoid tangling them. Like all the other

9

patients, I also have a phone and a remote control for the TV that I have to be careful of dropping. To top it off, my brain keeps lurching around in my skull, making me feel as though I'm falling.

As soon as I lift off the bed an alarm goes off, screaming out that I have broken the 'no leaving your bed without assistance' rule. By the time I'm creeping gingerly toward the commode, dragging my intravenous tubes and hiking up my hospital gown, I've peed all over. Then the nurses come in.

For some reason, they hate me. I'm beginning to believe they mean me harm. When Edward visits, I try to tell him. He always excuses them, gently reminding me that their job is hard. He doesn't share my fear that they might hurt me.

***

One of the doctors seems even crazier than the one who cut my socks. He has an alcoholic brother who is a doctor here as well. I hear from the nurses that this alcoholic brother has botched many operations. Lately he's been keeping mostly to the apartment just down the hall from my room that the two brothers share. I tell Edward about all this, but again, he defends the doctor brothers as having difficult jobs. He doesn't even believe they have an apartment down the hall.

I've been told that I have to live with the crazy doctor and his alcoholic brother in their apartment. I don't understand why I have to stay with them. "You need to be watched carefully!" they snapped at me when I

11

protested.

I'm in my bed that has been wheeled into their living room which looks just like a hospital room. The crazy doctor has a desk with a computer and printer on it. He spends a lot of time searching for my art that I have online. I watch him scroll through the poetry I've posted on various sites, and my drawings that I scanned and uploaded to my flicker account. He mumbles to himself as he does this.

From listening to him, I've figured out that he intends to hack into my computer so he can access my documents. In 'my docs', I have all my writing, photography and drawings, not to mention the pins and passwords to all my favorite sites. He intends to steal all of that. Also in 'my docs' is a folder with all my family's email addresses. He will find them and hack into their computers, get into their banking and rob them blind!

"Eureeka!" he shouts, bouncing in his seat. He's gotten in. Now I hear him reading aloud as he scrolls through all of my stories and poems. He's found my personal journal and is reading with great interest. So now he will know all about my past. He will use it against me I'm sure.

He's found the nude photos of me that Edward and I took together. He's printing them up and pinning them on the wall above his desk. I can see them from here.

I recognize the pen and ink drawing of a dog that Edward and I made a few years ago. The crazy doctor has chosen to pin it among the nudes of me, though I don't know how he got it, since it's never been scanned onto my computer.

He's excited about sculpture. "I'm an artist too!" he beams at me, apparently thrilled that we have this in common. He's decided to make a sculpture of me, but it's not going well. "It's because I'm not inspired!" he cries in frustration to his brother, slouched in his armchair across from my bed. "I'd much rather be sculpting *him* ..." he glances at me with a secretive smirk as he says this.

"Well then why don't you get him here and do it?" his brother suggests.

"I just might do that!" says the crazy doctor. He's animated now at the thought of sculpting this secret 'him'. I know they're talking about my boyfriend. Edward is in danger. The crazy doctor rushes out the door, his brother goes to bed. I am alone.

**

The crazy doctor is climbing back in through the window! I start screaming, but this just makes him move faster. He seems drunk. He lands with a thud on the floor and rushes to my bed. I scream louder. A group of nurses and a male orderly barge in through the door. They grapple with me to hold me down. "You're in a hospital!" they all clamor at me "We're trying to help you!"

The crazy doctor has a needle as long as my forearm, he's trying to insert it in my neck. I can't imagine it going in and not coming through the other side! I scream and fight and bite and kick, but in the end he injects me, swearing at me the whole time. He has it in for me, I've noticed. Now he'll hate me even more because I fought so hard. I'm terrified, and then I feel my senses falling away.

I must have been out for many hours. It feels like night time. The doctor is seated beside a wooden platform, working by lamplight, moving his hands over another man's face and body. The man is lying on his back on the platform. He's completely covered in plaster of paris, including his nose and mouth, the crazy doctor is massaging it in.

"You have to make air holes! He can't breathe!" I scream. I know that the man is Edward. He is being slowly smothered to death beneath that mask of clay.

The doctor pays no attention to me. I can tell that Edward is still alive. I scream at him "Ed! Do you believe me now?! I told you something was going on here and you didn't believe me, now look at you!" I'm crying and yelling at the same time. My heart is absolutely broken as I watch him die before me.

"Oh! I've lost him!" I shriek "Just when I was getting to know him, now he's gone! Oh dear God I've lost him." Tears are streaming down my face but no one seems to care. My heart is broken for Edward, and I'm mad at him for not believing me about this place. Now it's too late.

I must have slept, though I can't imagine how. When I woke, the crazy doctor was standing beside my bed. "I have something to show you." he said with barely suppressed excitement. I followed him to another room where there was an old fashioned tin tub. Edward was in the tub, naked, his flesh being consumed by the acid that had been poured in there. I stared in horror until much of him had been reduced to a skeleton, then I ran, sobbing, back to my bed.

I've spent hours watching the crazy doctor working on his sculpture of Edward. Now it's early morning, and the doctor has finished. He's prancing around, admiring his handiwork. He used Edward's skull as the armature. The sculpture of his head and shoulders is fixed to a stake, and there is a real carrot dangling from a string in front of Ed's mouth. The doctor is incredibly pleased. I can't believe Edward is really dead. My entire universe is empty.

... And there he is coming through the door! Edward is good as new, as though nothing at all happened to him. I have to touch his hand to believe it. He's come back from the dead. I ask him how he managed to survive the ordeal. He looks at me with concern and insists "Nothing happened to me!"

I'm at a loss. I point out the stolen photos pinned to the wall, I point to the sculpture of him that sits obviously right there on the doctor's desk. He's see's none of it.

***

I've learned that some of the nurses are meth addicts. Also some of the orderlies. One of the nurses is going out with one of the orderlies. I feel I can trust these two more than some of the other staff, because they're quite nice to me, but I know they're both meth addicts.

She's pregnant, and is

concerned because of her addiction - her six month old son is a water-head baby as a result. Now she has found out this pregnancy is a water-head baby as well. 'Paris' is also a meth addict and has two water-head babies.

The pregnant nurse has invited me to her apartment tonight for dinner. I don't want to go, because I'm afraid it's a plan to kill me. She was there when the crazy doctor stuck me with that foot long needle. But that doesn't necessarily mean she's one of the bad guys. Maybe she was just doing her job. Still, what if she and her boyfriend consider killing me 'just doing their jobs?' Can I trust anyone after what happened to Edward?

I'm at the pregnant nurse's apartment, along with her boyfriend, a few of the other nurses I recognize from the ward, and a few of the other orderlies. The water-head baby is in a carrier under the table.

I understand that the pregnant nurse is trying to keep the baby in shadows because she's embarrassed about his head which has a huge, veiny blob growing out of it. His eyes are swollen shut. I lay on the couch in my hospital gown with a blanket wrapped around me. I don't know why I'm here. The others are all seated at a long table nearby, ignoring me.

They're all getting high on meth. The orderly boyfriend is getting crazier by the minute. I realize he isn't as nice as I had thought. He stands up abruptly and points his finger at the baby who has now been placed, in his carrier, onto the table. "I want a new life!" he growls. "I want everything out!" he jabs his finger into the baby's chest "I'll throw this freak out first!"

He stomps out the sliding glass door to the small balcony. It's dark outside, and raining. I'm so scared. I know the higher he gets, the crazier he'll become. I feel completely frozen. My brain is whirling with panicky thoughts while on the outside, I probably look completely calm. I'm purposely keeping my face expressionless so that I don't betray the fact that I'm terrified.

He barks at his girlfriend to come out on the balcony. She looks nervously at everyone, then meekly steps out onto the porch where her boyfriend orders her to strip. He's yelling at her "You're Fat!" he shouts, backhanding her "You're stupid! You gave me a fucked up monster baby!" He punches her.

The other nurses rush out to the balcony. They're trying to protect her, but he pushes them away. I see him take out a tazer from the holster he wears around his waist. The nurses all gasp. His pregnant girlfriend just stands mute. Frozen.

All the orderlies have tazers. They like to shoot them off outside the hospital. Now the orderly is taking aim at his girlfriend. He shoots her in the upper thigh. She doesn't make a sound.

He shoots her again and again in the same place, all the while yelling at her that she's a fat bitch who ruined his life. She's weeping now. She sounds so terribly, terribly broken. The other nurses come inside, subdued. One of them hurries to the bathroom, crying, muttering "So much sadness! So much sadness! I'm so tired of all the sadness!"

***

I've been here all night, listening to the orderly abuse his girlfriend out on the balcony. I see through the window that the sun is beginning to come up. Now he's barging around the apartment, demanding more drugs. There isn't any left. His girlfriend runs, weeping, past him. There's a black hole in her leg where he shot her repeatedly with the tazer. There's smoke coming out of the hole.

Her boyfriend finds some meth, and now he's shouting for some stuff to mix it with. I believe he wants some kind of gas. There is none. Finally he stomps out to the car and takes some gas from the tank. Now he's back, mixing it together with the meth and one of those little blue balls you put in the vacuum cleaner to kill fleas, that he has crushed up.

He drinks some of it, and pours the rest into an enema bag. Then he goes out to the balcony, pulls down his pants and lays down on his side. He shoves the enema hose into his ass and suddenly lets loose a great cry as diarrhea roars out and vomit spews from his wide open mouth. Everything all over himself and the porch.

I hear a burst of electric popping. He's shooting himself with the tazer. There's another explosion of diarrhea and puking. Diarrhea - puking - tazer blasts - diarrhea - puking - tazer blasts ... his girlfriend looks at the others, embarrassed. "He really likes that." she tells them.

I've been listening to the nurses whispering about me in the hall all evening. 'Paris' is on shift again for tonight, as well as the skinny, junkie looking nurse who keeps her thin, greasy hair wound in two little pin curls on either side of her head. This one is especially crazy. I'm terrified of her. She, of all the nurses, is the most capable of killing me. "Tonight!" I hear the nurses promise each other, flashing knowing looks at me "It's definitely happening tonight."

I've been screaming for hours. The nurses and orderlies keep coming at me with needles. One time I saw that 'pin curls' has a knife. Each time they come in, I fight them off. They huddle together a few feet from my bed, whispering about how to kill me. "Should we take her to the basement?" They ask each other.

They keep threatening to tie my wrists to the side-bars of my bed, but I beg them off. I pretend I'm going to be quiet and so they relent and go away.

I'm a little confused - if they're planning to murder me, why do they so easily give in when I beg to not be tied down? Why haven't they seriously attacked me yet? What's going on? I'm so terrified I don't know what to do with myself.

I've suddenly remembered the phone that every patient is given for use while we're here. I could call 911! I press the buttons with shaking fingers. When a policeman answers, I frantically whisper my name and where I am. I tell him they're trying to kill me.

I need help immediately. I need desperately to convey to him the enormity of my situation. I see one of the nurses coming in. I begin to scream as loud and long as I can, right into the phone.

For some reason, the nurse doesn't take away my phone. Why are they letting me get away with it? Are they afraid of me, even as they try to kill me?

"Marian." the nurse croons "You're in a hospital. We're trying to help you." She sounds and looks so concerned. I know it's all a pretense. I heard them talking about killing me! Don't they realize I heard them?

"Why are you doing this?" I beg the nurse.

She gazes at me with her blank, robotic face and murmurs "Doing what?" She seems like a sleepwalker. All the nurses do tonight. Either they're acting this way on purpose to freak me out, or they've all been drugged. Either way, I'm in great trouble.

'Pin curls' comes in. I begin to scream again. She will kill me with her bare hands if she wants to. She's very skinny, but I have a bad feeling she's abnormally strong. She's just standing there beside another nurse. Both of them staring at me, waiting for their opening. I'm screaming and screaming. They've left the room.

I hear a sudden male voice coming from behind the curtain around the bed next to mine. It's the orderly who tazed his pregnant girlfriend. He's calling someone on his cell. "You better come quick." he snaps into the phone. "There's a little girl here who's gonna be running for her life in a minute."

What a relief! He knows what's going on and he's bringing help. He gives instructions in rapid Spanish, then switches again to English "I'll go check out the basement, you climb in the window here and wait." He hangs up. I don't see him leave, so I lean over and move the curtain. There's no one there. He must have slipped out through a door that I don't see from this angle.

I can hear him now, moving around in the basement two floors below. I know that 'pin curls' and some of the other nurses have gone down to the basement as well. I know that they have knives, maybe even guns. I hope the orderly has his taser.

I'm straining to hear if the friend should come in through the window, and listening for sounds from the basement. As well, I'm listening for sirens that will tell me the cops are here.

Now I hear it! The friend has climbed in through the window. He's getting into the bed there on the other side of the curtain. I assume he's waiting until the time is right, to go and help his friend in the basement.

The nurses are creeping up on the orderly from their basement hiding place behind some stacked boxes! The basement is very dim. There are storage things piled all over the place. The orderly doesn't see or hear the nurses coming. I scream as loud as I can "Watch out! They're right behind you!"

Luckily this alerts him and he spins around just in time. There's a ferocious struggle, then the orderly is screaming. He's been stabbed. The nurses all run for a staircase I hadn't noticed before. It's dusty and filled with cobwebs. It leads to a dingy room where the nurses hide.

I can't believe the orderly's friend hasn't moved from the bed. Didn't he hear the commotion down there? Is this man the only ally I have now? If that's the case, I'm doomed. I reach across again and move the curtain. The man is cowering beneath the blanket. "How can you just lie there while your friend is being stabbed?!" I demand. He pulls the blanket closer.

I call 911 again. "Why haven't you sent anyone?! I cry to the cop who answers "The nurses have already attacked an orderly, I think he's dead! I'm next! Please come now! Please!"

The cop doesn't seem fazed, just calmly asks my name and where I am. I can't remember the

32

name of the hospital. "I think it's called 'Memorial.'" I yell, "Or 'Sutter' they keep changing their name. I'm on the second floor - or is it the first? I'm not sure, they keep moving me around." I babble on and on. He tells me calmly that they'll be here as soon as they can. I don't believe they'll come at all.

Now I hear them! Sirens. It sounds like at least a half dozen police cars. They screech into the parking lot outside my window and then just sit there! Finally they appoint one young rookie to come into the hospital and see what's going on. They obviously don't think it's a big deal. I call 911 again to tell the front desk to order these cops to get moving.

I've called 911 over and over again, but get nothing but ringing. They're not answering. Once it was picked up and I heard some of the nurses on the other end, giggling "She thinks she's calling 911." they snickered. I don't know what to make of it.

I lean across again to pull the curtain back from the bed next to mine. The man is still just lying there under the blanket. I whisper as loud as I can - I must keep quiet so he isn't noticed by the staff here. Even though he seems to be wimping out on this rescue mission, he's my only hope now. "Please help me! Please help your friend! Get me out of here I don't want to die!" He just ignores me.

A couple of nurses come in again and pull me away from the curtain. "That man is sick." they tell me "Don't bother him he's trying to sleep." So they know he's here and think he's a patient. That's good news at least. Won't they be surprised when he leaps out and saves the day!

The nurses discuss the police outside, not caring that I can hear them … glad that I can hear them. They're using this opportunity to let me know that no matter what I do, it won't be enough to save myself. "What do you think will happen?" one nurse asks the other.

"She's talking to him now." the other one answers, meaning 'Paris' is talking with the lone rookie the police sent in. I know she will easily convince the cop to tell his buddies there's nothing going on here. The nurse seconds my thought "She can handle it no problem." The two nurses laugh. It's night outside. The revolving lights from the police cars stream in through my window, following the nurses as they walk calmly out the door.

I know I have to do

something quickly before 'Paris' convinces the rookie that all is well. I sit up in bed and scream as loud as I possibly can. Over and over again "I'm on the second floor! Help! The orderly is in the basement! He's been wounded! The nurses are hiding in a secret room down there!"

Now I realize that the nurses have blocked the door to my room with lumber. They've nailed it shut. But I see there's a cupboard against the wall beside my bed. I hadn't known it was there before. I know there's a door behind it. The police will have to break through the cupboard to rescue me. I scream out this new information.

I hear the nurses running up the hall toward my room, there are male voices among them. My supper sits untouched on the bed tray, I'm going to throw it at them as soon as they appear. I've never been good at sports. Most likely I won't even hit them, but I have to try.

They arrive as a group, crowding through the doorway which is no longer barricaded, clamouring at me. I grab a yogurt cup and hurl it as hard as I can. It glances off the doorway, and splatters all over 'Paris' who is in front. "Oh!" she squeals as she jumps back. I fling a bun at them, and some meat. They're scrambling to get out of the way, as though I was throwing hand grenades.

Now I hear the police slamming their car doors and running towards the hospital. They have dogs as well. I hear a few of the cops trying to break down the door into the basement. Now I hear the wounded orderly. He's not dead, thank goodness. He's shuffling toward the door to let the police inside, moaning in pain with each step.

The police are inside now, in the basement. They're shouting for the nurses to come out. I hear the nurses clamoring, all crying as though they were victims. "He stabbed himself!" 'Pincurls' insists, indicating the bleeding orderly "He came after us so we hid!"

I yell out that the nurses are lying, repeating my directions to get to my room, but it's difficult because there are five nurses in my room now, all taking turns to run to my bed and try to shut me up. They're always very gentle, never forcing me. I don't understand why they're so hesitant to kill me immediately, but I won't question it. I think it's because they're afraid of me. That gives me hope.

Three male orderlies have come into my room. They have their tazers out. They're all high on meth, swaggering around like gangsta's, creeping up to the window to see all the cop cars with their lights flashing.

Some of the cops are outside with the dogs, among them, a golden retriever. I know he's one of the dogs that are brought here to visit the patients.

The orderlies are excited. The nurses are gushing with admiration for them as they climb out onto the window ledge and aim their tazers at the police. The police warn each other. Then there's a rat!tat!tat!tat! as one of the orderlies shoots and his friends join in. The police fire back. It sounds like war out there. At least while the orderlies are shooting at the cops, they and the nurses will be distracted from killing me. I only hope the dogs are okay.

I hear a group of policemen and one police woman running around inside the hospital. They can't seem to find my floor. What in the world is wrong with them? Somehow I expected American cops to be savvier than this. I realize I'm in the hands of a bunch of yokels. It's up to me to save my own life. But I don't think I can. I'm not strong enough and I'm grossly outnumbered. I can only hope for a miracle.

'Paris' has come in. She tells the other nurses that the golden retriever has been shot, and is lying in his own blood outside. She doesn't know if he's alive or dead. Paris is concerned about the dog. "I'm going out there." she announces "I'm getting that dog in here so he can be saved"

I haven't heard anything from the basement in some time. I don't know what has happened to the wounded orderly. His friend has defected to the other side. He's out there on the window ledge now with his tazer, shooting at the cops.

The police have sent two more of their own to knock on the hospital's locked front door and try to talk some sense into the staff here. 'Paris' immediately volunteers to talk with them. "Don't step over the threshold." one of the other nurses cautions her "They can't arrest you if you're still standing inside this building. They can't come in unless you invite them either." 'Paris' repeats all this information to herself, her eyes are bright with excitement. Then she scampers downstairs to pull open the heavy, wooden front door.

"Hi!" I hear her bright voice. "I was just wondering if you'd like something to eat? Some pie and hot chocolate? You must be so cold out there!"

The two cops chuckle and ask to be allowed inside. 'Paris' says no, but stays standing just within the door, making polite conversation with them. They're acting as though nothing strange is going on. I'm worried that maybe they're not acting at all, but actually believe everything is under control.

I wish I could scream, but the orderlies are all in here with their tazers. Maybe I should scream anyway, what do I have to lose?

I scream and scream. The nurses rush to quiet me. The orderlies glare at me, like they can't wait to taze me. I stop screaming, babbling that I won't do it again "Just don't tie me." I beg when one of the nurses suggests it to the others. I promise over and over and they leave me untied.

Everyone except for two orderlies has left my room for the moment. Now is my chance to escape. I don't know if I can make it, but I will try. I limp as fast as I can for the door. One orderly whirls around and snaps at his companion "We've got a runner!" They both rush to grab me. I've gotten the door open, I'm halfway out into the hall. The orderlies are grappling with me, peeling my fingers from the door, dragging me away as I kick and scream. I've been tied down now.

Things are quiet outside. The cops are gone from the front door. 'Paris' has successfully turned them away. She comes upstairs, laughing at the way she offered them pie. The others crowd around her, praising her. She remembers the dog again. "I'm going out there now." She turns on her heel and leaves.

The other nurses and the orderlies all rush to the window. "She's gonna get herself shot!" they exclaim to each other. The man who betrayed his wounded friend and myself says he'll cover her. When she appears outside, running at a crouch among the police cars toward the wounded retriever, he opens fire. The police fire back. 'Paris' reaches the dog and drags him to safety. The other nurses let her inside. Everyone is so proud of 'Paris'.

The orderlies have come back in from the window ledge and closed the windows. They and the nurses have left the room. I am alone. I find I'm no longer tied up. Sliding carefully out of my bed, I creep to the window and lift the blind. Several cops have snuck around the back of the building and are sliding furtively along the wall beneath my window. They don't see me looking down on them through the glass. I know I mustn't signal them because it would put everyone in more danger.

They gather together and one of them reads from a list of names – the patients they're here to save. My name is last to be mentioned. "So she's still here." The cop murmurs, his voice cracking with emotion "She's been trying to get help for ages!" I feel calmer now that I've heard this. People know I'm here.

It's getting near Christmas. A couple of days ago, a group of old men from a hospital run charity came by with little   Christmas decorations they had put together. They very sweetly came to each bed in turn to ask if the patient wanted one to hang above their bed. Some of the patients said 'No', but most said 'Yes'. I have one - hanging beside the 'Kicker' sign tacked to the wall above my pillow.

I earned that sign when I kicked out at one of the orderlies. Ed was there and saw it. He didn't know what I knew - the orderly was trying to poison me. After I kicked at him, the orderly duct-taped my wrists to the safety bars around my bed, so tight my circulation felt cut off. I tried to bite the tape off, but Edward stopped me, and helped me loosen it a little.

Actually I like that orderly. He moves up and down the hall with trays of food, and helps out wherever he's needed. He's always very patient with me. I found out he's not really an orderly - he's a patient here. He told me he's doing this unpaid job to get on the good side of the doctors and nurses so they will release him. "We're all just trying to get home." he said sadly "Just like you."

I've noticed he sometimes gets beaten up for no reason, by three burly men that the 'crazy doctor' calls up. "Get Steve" he'll bark at a nurse nearby. And there will come Steve and the two other stooges, barreling up the hall and grabbing the 'pretend orderly' and hauling him away. I hear his cries,

47

but then, when it's over and he's back with his trolley, he acts like nothing at all happened. I worry about him.

I don't blame him for trying to poison me with that needle. I know he was just following orders so he wouldn't get beaten. I'm sure he doesn't blame me for kicking him either.

***

Last night I tried to pull out my catheter. I kept pulling and pulling until I had about two feet out. I could see something metal appearing, but it wouldn't come out any further. So now I have two feet of intestines hanging out of me. I try to roll it all up inside my panties, but it keeps falling out. When I pee, it falls into the commode.

I've been moved to another room. It's quite a large room with many other patients, both male and female. When the nurse wheeled me into this room on my bed, she introduced me to an intimidating looking nurse "This is Hilda, she's in charge of this room. Don't give her any trouble and you'll be just fine!" She and Hilda exchanged looks *'She's a handful, but we'll soon show her who's boss!'* their expressions said.

The other nurse left, and I was, for all intents and purposes, alone with Hilda since the other patients appeared to be asleep. She pointed out the medicine cabinet near my bed "This is where I keep all the medications." she announced briskly "As well as the pain killers." she darted a suspicious look at me "I keep the key for the drawer right here." she

49

picked up a key hanging from a string on the wall, and inserted it into the lock, opening the drawer and taking out some pill bottles "I keep track of how many painkillers are in here, so don't you try and steal any!" She dropped the bottles back into the drawer, locked it and hung up the key.

She pointed to an open door, showing a small room inside. There was a cot with a young man lying on it. "That's my son." she snapped. "He's a meth addict so I make him sleep in there. If you become a meth addict I'll make you sleep in there as well!" She glared at me. Glared at the sleeping body of her son.

***

Tonight the 'pretend orderly' came to my bed and told me the 'crazy doctor' wanted to see me. I knew what it was about. I know the 'crazy doctor' regularly invites the nurses to pose nude for him. They do it willingly. I have been ordered to do it against my will.

The 'pretend orderly' helps me into the shower, and after, helps me back into my hospital gown. I'm wearing a huge pad in case of 'accidents', the bandage on my leaky side is soggy, my intestines are falling out of my snatch. I have to keep pushing them back in. Why on earth would anyone want me to pose nude in this condition? "I've never felt so unsexy in my life." I say.

Now I'm tied to a chair. The 'pretend orderly', Hilda's addict son, about six nurses, and a handful of patients I know are meth addicts, are seated on the other side of my room, watching me. They've replaced the beds on that side with several rows of chairs. They're all smoking meth. We're all waiting for the 'crazy doctor' to arrive with his camera.

Hilda's son is worried she will catch him smoking meth. He keeps darting glances at the door. I watch them smoking, and decide I might as well be an addict too, so I ask for some. Hilda's son tells me to wait. One of the patients sticks up for me "She could probably use it." he says, but Hilda's son has smoked it all. There is no more.

Hilda walks in, taking in the scene with one resigned glance. Her son is so high he's no longer worried. "Go ahead." Hilda says to all of them. "I don't care anymore." She doesn't seem to care either that I'm tied up here in this chair when I should be in bed.

***

We've been here for hours. The doctor finally appeared, and announced that he didn't feel like any photography tonight after all. I was untied, and the nurses, orderlies, patients and the doctor all seated in their rows of chairs, silently watched as I arranged my intestines in a coil on the floor in front of me. I tried to pull them out some more - I really pulled hard. More came out. They've tied me up again now.

Now Edward is here. But he doesn't seem to notice I'm tied to this chair. He ignores the crowd of meth addled hospital staff and patients. He doesn't even comment on the fact of my intestines on the floor.

A man and a woman, with a small Chinese boy are walking past my chair - visitors for one of the patients. "Please don't step on my intestines!" I call out quickly.

The group keeps walking forward. I cry out again "Please don't step on my intestines!" To my relief, they stop then.

The woman says kindly "We won't step on your intestines." They take a wide, exaggerated step over them, except for the little boy, who pretends he's going to jump on them. I cry out and the woman calls him away. After a short time, they all leave the way they came, stepping carefully over my intestines. Edward is looking at me warily. I'm not sure why.

***

They've decided to remove the useless catheter. They also stitched the hole in my side that is still leaking. Now I have two stitched holes in my belly - this accidental one, and the one from the original outside catheter, or maybe it's from when they drained my belly. I can't keep track of all that is going on with me. For some reason they chose at the last minute to put in yet another catheter. This one is apparently better than the others, but they said that last time.

***

One of the friendlier nurses has offered to take me for a short walk up and down the hall. She attaches a wide belt around my waist, with a cloth handle for her to hang onto, so I don't fall. She keeps talking about a former ninety year old patient who insisted on getting her exercise every day while she was here.

"She would literally do the splits against this wall here." The nurse exclaims several times. I realise she's trying to make me feel guilty for not being able to do the same. Blaming me for spending so much time in my bed. I don't like her anymore.

She asks me what's happening to make me scream and lash out. I tell her some of the staff is trying to kill me. I tell her I'm acting out of great fear for my life, not because I'm a mean person.

She says I'm having hallucinations. "It's from your alcoholism." she tells me "There's a lot of ammonia in your brain, we're trying to get it out with meds."

I know she's lying. She's making excuses so I won't accuse the staff. So I'll go along with them when they try to kill me, telling myself 'this is not real, it's just a hallucination' which will make it easier for them.

***

The people with the visitor animals have come again. The man in the bed across the room from me has the big golden retriever with him - the one who was wounded in the shootout, and has since recovered. There is also a small poodle, a chicken, some cats, a couple of rabbits and I don't know what else in bed with the man across the room. He's persuaded the hospital staff that he's the best choice for having all the animals with him day and night. The rest of us are apparently not to be trusted with them.

No one except me knows that the man tortures the animals. One of the cats has been tied up inside his pillow case and is probably dead by now. I'm afraid to tell any of the staff because they never believe anything I say, and telling them might bring harm to the remaining animals. So I just lay here in my bed and glare at the man, letting him know I'm aware of what kind of a nut case he is. I hate him for hurting those animals. I feel responsible for them since I'm the only one who seems to know what's going on, but I feel helpless to intervene.

Once when Ed was visiting, I started to tell him about the animals. I hesitated to tell him about the abuse because he doesn't seem to recognize what is going on here and always comes to the defense of the staff.

I compromised by simply telling him that the animals come

around to visit the patients. I intended to ease up to the subject of the abuse gradually. But he stopped me by saying it isn't possible that animals are brought here. I pointed out the retriever on the bed across the room. He insisted there was no dog there.

Now the creep across the room is holding up the poodle by the neck and grinning at me. In the hope that he might not hurt the dog more if I just ignore him, I lift my magazine to my face. I'm frozen, afraid to move for fear that he will kill the dog.

***

It's night time again. I dread the night because there is less staff, so the ones who remain are free to torture and try to kill me and the other patients.

There's a husband and wife team who live in a trailer on the hospital grounds. Their job is to come in after dark to make sure the night staff are not running amok. They wander around with their flashlights, peering around corners. But they never do anything else. Just look around with grave expressions, and then leave. I believe they're afraid of the staff. They're certainly no help to me. I don't even bother calling out to them anymore.

The patient across the room has killed a rabbit by twisting its neck. He skinned it and made a huge pair of mittens and stuffed a few dead mice in the mittens while wearing them. I saw him kill the chicken and stuff its dismembered body under his mattress the other day. I'm amazed the staff here don't smell it!

Now he's trying to cut the retriever's stomach open. The dog is resisting. A group of nurses comes in and surrounds his bed. I'm glad they've caught him red handed, now at least the remaining animals will be saved. But they don't seem to care at all about the animals. They ask him what he's doing and he tells them he wants to stuff all the live animals into the dog.

One of the nurses - a tall, muscular woman with short blond hair and wire framed glasses, grabs one of the rabbits "I'll show you how it's done." she says with barely suppressed excitement. The other nurses watch her in silent admiration as she grips the rabbit's ear and yanks back hard, grimacing with the effort. The ear and some of the skin from that side of the rabbit's head tear away with a wet, bloody RIP!

The man in the bed cuts the rest of the way across the retriever's belly and the nurse thrusts the mutilated rabbit inside. Together, she and the man fit the remaining animals in as well. The man stitches up the wound. I can see the animals moving around in there. The retriever is moaning.

I'm in shock. Inside my head I'm screaming in fear for the animals and myself. It's up to me to save the animals but I'm just lying here, screaming inside my head.

One of the nurses has discovered the dismembered chicken under the man's mattress and pulled it all out, looking at the other nurses with a questioning expression. They reach under his bedding and find other animal body parts, they check his mittens.

They seem only mildly concerned. Even the still living retriever with its belly stuffed with dead and dying animals fails to faze the nurses. They confiscate some of the body parts but leave him with several, including the mittens, though they remove the dead animals from inside them. He puts them on again and waves at me.

***

A patient in my room is waiting for her husband to arrive and take her home. She's arguing with the nurses about some money that is owed. The nurses have called the crazy doctor and now they're holding a discussion in the hall. "We can't let her out until she pays up!" the doctor exclaims "It's thirty-five dollars!"

Without warning, the woman speeds out of the room in her

wheelchair and parks herself near the front doors, her hands poised on the wheels, ready to rush out the door at the first opportunity. The doctor and nurses hurry after her, surrounding her in her chair. They're trying to pretend all is normal. Stalling while they figure out how to stop her from escaping. She laughs and jokes with them, as though they were all friends.

Then suddenly the front door opens and the woman whooshes out and is gone, leaving the astonished hospital staff behind. One of the nurses picks up a crumpled piece of paper the woman threw to the floor as she made her escape, and reads it aloud. 'Happy fucking birthday!'

Another patient in my room has been discharged today as well. He's waiting for someone to take him home. I envy him. The nurses told him he can't leave until his friends arrive, but he can drink all he wants in the meantime. One of the nurses went to the liquor store to buy him a case of beer.

Now he's sitting on his bed, drinking. I'm afraid of him. He seems nice, but I know he's one of the group of patients who are meth addicts. He might get drunk and try to kill me. I hope his friends arrive soon and take him away.

The nurse who mutilated the rabbit comes at me with a needle. She grips my arm and injects me with something. I'm afraid to fight her off. I'm terrified of her. She's probably injected poison into my veins, but I'm too scared to do anything more than glare at her, trying to convey my deep disgust with her for her act of gross animal abuse. She ignores me. She obviously knows she won't be punished for what she did. They're all crazy in this place. I will die here.

***

I'm lying beside Edward on a narrow bunk bed. We're on the top bunk, on our stomachs, our hands are tied behind our backs. We've twisted our heads, awkwardly, so we can see the room beyond.

It's a tiny, dingy, cluttered apartment. Threadbare clothes and sheets hang from ropes stretched across the low ceiling. I can't move my head enough to see, but I sense the apartment is just one room. The cramped quarters feel claustrophobic.

The kitchen is in one corner, with a large, rusty box for a stove. The box has a hole cut into it near the bottom, where a Chinese woman I recognize as one of the nurses, is shoving in pieces of wood. There are numerous tin cans suspended by wires over the stove. The Chinese nurse drops pieces of meat into one of the tins as she barks at another Chinese woman I don't recognize "We have to hurry! We have to get to work!" I assume they are room-mates. I notice a small grimy window beside the stove. I see that it's raining. I know now that we are in China.

Edward has a phone. He's untied himself somehow, though I'm still tied up. I resent him for not untying me. He's making frenzied calls to lawyers in America, whispering into the phone so the Chinese nurse and her room-mate won't hear.

And then he leaves! Just jumps down off the bunk and waltzes out the door! I try to come after him, but my hands are tied. Edward flaps his hand at me to stay put. The Chinese nurse rushes up to me, barking at me to stay in bed. Neither she nor her room-mate seem to care that Edward is getting away. Why are they letting him get away and not me? Why did he leave me here?! Come to think of it, why was he even here? He isn't a patient at the hospital.... Suddenly I'm struck with the new knowledge that he is, in fact, a patient. I feel betrayed. Why didn't he tell me?

The Chinese nurse has a needle, and a very determined look on her face. I'm screaming at her to stay away, yanking at the straps around my wrists. Why oh why didn't Edward untie me?! I hope he got through to someone. The nurse has jabbed the needle in. I assume I've been poisoned.

***

I'm lying on my stomach with my hands tied behind my back and my head turned to see the Chinese nurse and her room-mate leaving for work. I hope Edward is okay. He doesn't know what he's up against with these people. How will he get back home from China without any shoes? He doesn't even know the language.

I know the poison will begin to work very soon. I have to do something. Suddenly my hands are no longer tied, and I have a laptop here on the bunk bed with me. I begin to type a long email to my sister in Canada....

'This is a strange and confusing story, but please believe me every word is true. I need your help desperately. This hospital is a

criminal place. They've now kidnapped Edward and me and taken us here to China. I think they're connected with Chinese gangs. Edward and I need lawyers right away. Will you please contact Peter and Mary? Tell them our lives are in danger. Erase all your banking information, tell everyone in our family to do the same - one of the doctors has hacked into my computer, he probably has your email, and can probably get into your banking. Change all your passwords! Tell Peter to come with his sister immediately! I'm sorry to alarm you....'

***

I'm back in the hospital, but I'm still in China. Amazingly, the hospital has recreated my ward exactly as it was in California, only it's here! In China!

I'm sitting on a chair in the hall with several other patients. Beside me is a man in a wheelchair, with a metal plate in his head. I've seen him here before, he's been in the hospital at least as long as I have. He's very quiet and depressed, but he seems to like me. A chair has been taken out of the row, to accommodate his wheelchair. I see that his pants are ripped down the thigh and a terrible scar is showing through. I see dried blood. I wonder why they didn't give him clean hospital clothes.

The front desk is directly in front of us. Everyone is bustling around; nurses, doctors and patients. Patients form a line in front of the doctor who cut my socks. Other than that one incident, he's always seemed more

71

normal than the other staff here.

As each patient reaches him, he or she immediately begins babbling desperately about needing a place to stay. They hadn't expected to end up here in China, they don't know the language, they have no shoes, no food, they are homeless. They want to go home to California. He keeps telling them to be patient. He hands them a paper with addresses, where, he says, they might be able to stay. He makes phone calls. He looks very tired.

I ask the 'metal plate man' what's going on. He tells me to be patient. I tell him I have nowhere to go. I have no shoes. I don't know the language. I wave to the doctor "I have no place to go!" I yell furiously "I have no shoes! I don't even know the language! How am I supposed to get back to the

States?!'"

The doctor ignores me. What is *wrong* with these people?! I yell again "What's wrong with you people?!" A few patients look my way. The doctor ignores me. I thought he, at least, was nice. Maybe he *is* one of the bad guys. He's here in China, after all, in this recreated hospital ward that was all done in such secret even the U.S. doesn't know of its existence! I know this now.

I also know that they're working on another recreated ward in India. They plan to kidnap Edward and me to that place next. I have to find out what happened to him. I turn to 'Metal plate man' "Have you seen my boyfriend?" I can't divulge Ed's name because I believe he doesn't want the hospital to know it.

'Metal plate man' finally turns

to me after I ask several times. His voice is very quiet "I'll tell you the way to make friends in this place." he says. I nod for him to go on. "You start with a little joke, something like this ..." and he launches into a long-winded spiel half of which I can't understand. I assume I'm supposed to laugh, since he said it was a joke. But I'm too pissed off about this China situation. I don't see how I'll ever get back home, I'll probably die here. Edward may already be dead. No one will ever know what happened to us.

'Metal plate man' is winding up his joke. He looks at me to see if I understand. I say "That's a good way to make friends, thank you for telling me, I'll definitely use that." He keeps searching my face "I understand." I tell him firmly "I understood what you said." He looks away without a word. I hope I wasn't too sharp with him. Now I feel guilty.

"Have you seen my boyfriend?" I ask him again after a while. He ignores me. I tap his shoulder "Have you seen my boyfriend? I have to know how he is, *please* help me!"

He looks at me tiredly, and motions for me to follow him down the hall. "You shouldn't be talking about this stuff out here. Stop talking about it."

He's very kindly. I believe he is my friend. He's in the same boat as me. I know that he is being tortured just like Edward and me. I shuffle beside him in his wheelchair to his room. He gets into bed and makes as though to go to sleep. I'm standing in his open doorway. *"Please!* " I beg. "Tell me what happened to my boyfriend?"

Suddenly he gestures to the man on a bed next to his. The man is lying with his face to the wall. 'Metal plate man' taps him on the shoulder and the man rears around to look at me. The man's face is a bloated, burnt orange blob. It's Edward. They've mutilated his face somehow. I let out a loud gasp and Ed falls back down onto his pillow. 'Metal plate man' flaps his hand at me to go away. I return to my chair in the hall. At least Edward is alive. Unrecognizable, but alive.

I have to pee, and I'm tired. I want to pee and go to bed, but I'm stuck here in this hard chair in the hall with everyone milling around, furious and confused at finding themselves here in China. I'm obviously not going to get any help unless I make a stink.

I stand up again and start yelling "I need a place to sleep! I'm dead tired, I walked all the way from that nurse's apar...." the Chinese nurse bustles up to me. I turn to her and lower my voice "I walked from your apartment, I have no shoes and my socks are all worn out and I have to pee." She tells me to sit back down on the chair. "Good Grief! I have to pee *now*! And I need some shoes, can't you see that?! And I'm tired, I need a bed, I don't even have a bed, can't you see that?!" I'm crying now.

She tells me kindly to come with her into one of the rooms nearby, but I'm pissed off again "I don't have any shoes! What's the matter with you?!" I've followed her to the room, stopping just inside the doorway, yelling at her.

"So, you think we should give

you some shoes?" She sounds exasperated. I can't believe the way the staff around here treats us patients. They abuse us beyond belief and then lose their patience when we react. They really seem to think us patients are in the wrong. Like we're criminals.

I stand with my hands on my hips "Yes!" I sneer at her, sticking out one of my feet from underneath the long hospital gown I'm wearing "Preferably gold or silver plated!" I'm proud of myself for being so witty in these desperate circumstances.

The other patients are all silently gazing at the floor. "I need to pee!" I call to the nurse again, I guess you want me to just pee right here on the floor!" I stand with my legs apart, lift my gown a little and pretend I'm going to pee. Some of the patients turn lethargically to watch.

The Chinese nurse hustles me into the room and points to a bed. "You can sleep in my bed." she says. I had no idea she slept here! I guess it's because her apartment is so far away from the hospital, she needs to stay here sometimes. I feel honored that she is allowing me to sleep in her bed. I wonder why she's willing to do it? Are we friends?

Maybe that's why she allowed Edward and me to stay at her apartment last night. But why did she leave us tied up if she's a friend? Maybe she doesn't understand that it's wrong what they're doing to us. She does, after all, live in a very small village here in China. They obviously do things very differently here.

She leaves the room. Suddenly I don't have to pee

anymore. I want something more to wear. There's a dresser against the wall with a mirror above it. I look at myself in the mirror. This is the first time in weeks that I've seen myself. I look haunted and very thin. My long, uncombed hair caught up in a tangled bun.

I open one of the drawers and choose a sheet from among others, wrapping it around myself. The Chinese nurse comes in and rushes up to me. "What are you doing? I thought you wanted to sleep!" She's upset that she caught me looking in her dresser drawers.

I just wanted to look at myself in the mirror." I stammer, embarrassed that I was caught snooping.

"There's no mirror there!" she snaps, looking at me like I'm crazy. I can't believe it. Everybody here keeps lying about what is and what is not here! How can I fight against this?

I feel exhausted, and start to walk toward the bed. The nurse grabs the sheet off of me "Don't wear something like that around here!" she whispers fiercely, darting a nervous look towards the open doorway. I suddenly think I understand.

"Oh!" I say in a loud whisper "Is this a house of prostitution?" I say 'house of prostitution' instead of 'whorehouse' because I've finally realized it's probably best if I'm extremely polite while here in China. I don't know the customs and don't want to insult anyone. She ignores me and puts me into her bed.

"Where are we?" I ask her. She looks confused. "What country?" I explain.

"We're in California! In Santa

Rosa!" she sounds amazed at me. I give her a quizzical look. How is it she doesn't know we're in China?

"We're in Santa Rosa now?" I ask. She tells me 'Yes. Just like we always were.' I understand now. Just as this ward was magically transplanted in China, and Ed and me and all the other patients transported there, so they have now returned us all to the States. I pull up the covers and fall asleep almost immediately.

***

I've been asleep for hours, maybe even a whole day. I feel great. I'm well rested, and feeling cozy under the blankets. I feel a little bit awkward about being in the Chinese nurse's bed - she's a nurse and I'm just a patient, I'm worried she might think I'm messing up her sheets or something. But she did offer, after all. I settle down again against the soft pillows.

Ed walks in. He shows no sign of the ordeal, his face is unscarred. "You made it!" I cry out. I'm so relieved. He seems happy. He looks like he just had a shower and changed into brand new clothes. He looks like he just came from vacation. I'm glad he's okay, but I don't understand why he left me tied up in China. And why is he still so friendly with the doctors and nurses after what they did? Why was he allowed to escape and not me, and why does he, again, show no signs of trauma?

He doesn't even *remember* the atrocities that have happened. I hate to think it, but I wonder if he's in cahoots with the hospital staff and is just pretending he doesn't remember. Yet that makes no sense. If he doesn't care about me at all and so isn't bothered by what's being done to me, that would at least be an explanation, horrific as it is. But how is it that he doesn't even care what happens to *him*?

Another theory is that they're injecting him with something that makes him forget everything that has gone on. If that's the case, he'll continue to go like a lamb to slaughter every time, since he won't remember that there's any reason to be afraid. It's only a matter of time before they go too far and actually succeed in killing him. But there's nothing I can do.

I ask him questions, trying to find out how he made it, without mentioning China. I don't quite trust him somehow. I just know he'd say he was never in China and that makes me feel desperately frustrated, scared, and terribly alone in this horror show.

***

I'm back in my own room. I hear a commotion out in the hall, but I can't see from my bed. There are several voices, I recognize the crazy doctor's voice, and what sounds like my brother-in-law Peter, along with a female voice that I believe to be his sister; Mary, who is a lawyer.

I hear the doctor telling them both to leave at once "You'll be sorry if you don't!" the doctor warns. Peter's voice is assured as he begins to outline the reasons they have come to the hospital to get me. Then he begins to talk about God.

"I have a relationship with Jesus Christ." he offers quietly "Don't you think you would be a happier man if you accepted the Lord right now?" The doctor is becoming more and more enraged. I can't believe Peter is making things worse for me.

The crazy doctor has ordered one of the nurses to 'Go get Steve!' The nurse scurries off and a few minutes later I hear 'the three stooges' barging up the hall.

There are screams from Peter and Mary, thuds, cracks, laughter from Steve and his buddies, whooping and hollering "Wow! Did you see the way his head bounced off the wall?!" Mary weeping and pleading for them to 'Just let us go! *Please!'* Then I hear her being dragged into a room nearby and the door slammed shut. She's being beaten, and interrogated in there. I hear a sound like water splashing - I think they're trying to drown her. Her cries are heartbreaking.

Peter is now begging for them to just let them go. They're sorry they came. They won't try to save me again. They will go back to Canada. I feel terrible for him, but I'm also mad at him for coming without properly preparing. What is the problem with everybody? No one seems to understand the extent of the danger here. I'm in this totally alone.

***

Finally Peter and Mary are allowed to leave. I hear them staggering out the door. Steve comes into my room to speak with Hilda who had been listening to the fight with great excitement, though she couldn't bring herself to actually step out and see for herself. Steve is totally pumped from beating up my brother-in-law. "Man, we nearly *killed* the guy!" he practically jumps up and down in his excitement "Blood *everywhere!*" he crows. Hilda nods and smiles in approval.

Steve turns to me "I have a feeling you'll be next." he says with a tiny hint of regret in his voice, like he doesn't really want to hurt me but orders are orders. "I'll speak with the doctor and find out if he wants me to beat you up too. You were warned, you know."

Hilda smiles at me with rough sympathy. "Just try not to think about it. Maybe you'll be spared." she says kindly.

***

I'm sitting cross-legged on my bed, the other patients in the room are quiet. There are three nurses in the room, all sitting near my bed and talking with me. They're being very friendly. I know it's because I have this beating coming up. The nurses confirmed that the crazy doctor has demanded I be punished for sending the email that brought Peter and his sister here.

The nurses are trying to distract me by talking and joking with me as though we were girls at a slumber party. Despite my fear of the beating to come, I feel festive. In fact I feel like we *are* girls at a slumber party. I know we're not, it just feels that way.

Since it's near Christmas, I suggest we sing Christmas carols together. I feel brave for suggesting it because these nurses have been involved in some of the atrocities that take place here. I worry that they'll sneer at me, but they don't. We all sing together for a while, and then one of them asks me if I'm scared. I know she's talking about the beating to come. I tell her "Yes. I'm scared, I'm trying not to think about it." She and the other nurses look at me with admiration. I feel pretty proud of myself.

After a long time, another nurse comes in and tells me the doctor has decided I won't be beaten this time. I'm relieved of course, but I know it's just a 'stay of execution'. What will happen tonight? Or tomorrow or the next day? Have I survived this threat only to be killed during the next one?

What has happened with Peter and his sister? Will my

whole family hate me now? What if the crazy doctor steals all their money by hacking into their computers? Will my family blame that on me as well?

***

A new patient has been put into the bed next to mine. She's a middle aged woman. The nurses say to each other that she's dying.

As they're making her comfortable, a female doctor comes in. She's always been strict, but nice to me. She's upset because the dying woman turns out to be a friend of hers. She stands beside the woman's bed now, comforting her. She tells the other nurses she had planned to take a plane somewhere tonight, but she will stay instead. I'm relieved. With her here all night I'll be safe from the rest of the staff ... unless she turns out to be one of the bad guys after all. I've been fooled like that before.

The nurses stick needles in the woman and hook her up to an intravenous tube. With nothing more to do for her, they leave the room. It's night time, and quiet, the other patients are sleeping. I alone am awake with this poor dying woman. I wish I could go over to her to comfort her, but I'm intravenously attached. Also, I don't want to startle her by setting off the alarm that goes off every time I leave my bed. Instead, I quietly sing 'Amazing Grace' for her. Soon after, she passes away. The nurses come to remove her body.

***

Another of the nurses has invited me to her apartment for dinner tonight. She's quite plain and seems a little out of place, like she's not quite one of the group. She's friendly, but I'm terrified. I'm certain it's another plot to kill me, yet I know I have no choice but to go. If I don't go, I will be forced. Even the nice nurses seem to have no choice but to go along with these torture/execution plans.

I've seen new nurses come in here, treat me well when we're first introduced, then turn around and join the others when they're gossiping about me, or worse, trying to kill me. I believe the peer pressure in here is huge.

I'm lying on the couch in the plain nurse's living room, bundled in my hospital robe and blanket. She has invited two other nurses that I recognize from the ward.

93

They're all sitting together in the kitchen. I can see them from my spot. I can hear everything they're saying.

"The boys are bringing us some chicken for dinner." says the plain nurse. She sounds very excited. I wonder why she's so excited about chicken. Why did she invite me here? What are they planning to do to me? I'm lying here, frozen with terror. They mostly ignore me. The plain nurse is the only one of the three who deigns to acknowledge my existence. I smile at her, trying to act as though I don't know they're plotting my death. It would be dangerous to let on that I have this knowledge.

The 'boys' come in, stomping noisily on the floor with their boots. Three young Mexican men. I recognize two of them as orderlies in the hospital. One of them is the guy who tazed his pregnant girlfriend, apparently the other one is the boyfriend of the plain nurse who lives here. I don't recognize the third one. They all stand in front of me on the couch, staring, saying nothing.

They tell the three nurses to come outside in the dark parking lot. The plain nurse lets out a cheer "It's chicken catching time!" The other two nurses glance at her skeptically as they all follow 'the boys' out the door.

I can hear them out there, firing off their tazers in bursts of sharp staccato. They're all getting high on meth. When they get high enough they'll come in here and kill me. I'm lying here, waiting for the end.

After a long time, they all burst back into the apartment. The plain nurse is carrying two cases which she sets on the floor. She opens the door of each case and coaxes out two small chickens - one from each case. They wander sleepily across the floor. I know these people intend to kill the chickens and I know I must save them, but I don't know how. All I can do is lie here and hope for the best for all of us.

'The boys' are eyeing the prettier of the three nurses. They start flirting with her, one of them starts making out with her. They tell her to get her coat, she's coming with them. The plain nurse acts as though she's not hurt that her boyfriend is leaving with them and will likely fuck the nurse. "Be back soon for dinner! I'm making it special!" she calls out after them. "There's gonna be salad!" I feel embarrassed for her, but I hope the boys don't come back. Maybe my life has been spared this time.

The plain nurse and the remaining nurse are talking again in the kitchen. They're discussing how the chickens will be killed. The plain nurse gets up suddenly from her chair and marches across the floor to one of the chickens. Plucking it up from the floor, she looks into its face and croons "Look at your sleepy eyes!" Then she shoves it into the microwave and slams the door.

I know I should cry out. I am an animal lover, damn it! This is a test to see if I can be counted on to save the animals. But I'm afraid for my own life. I fail the test by remaining silent as the nurse sets the timer and turns the microwave on. I can see inside the microwave's bright interior. The chicken is sitting there quite calmly, going round and round, letting out a small cluck every once in a while. I watch, frozen, weeping inside.

The chicken is growing alarmed. She lets out a sudden scream, tries to fly and explodes. The plain nurse grins at her friend who does not grin back. She looks disgusted. I realize that the plain nurse is trying to impress her co-worker. She doesn't know that she has failed completely in this attempt. I feel a bit sorry for her. I know what it's like to be an outsider.

She takes a plate to the microwave and paws out the mess onto it. The microwave is awash with blood and gore. She walks across to the other nurse and places the plate with reverence onto the counter between them "Have some!" she offers generously.

Her friend is appalled. The plain nurse scoops out a hunk from the remains and shovels it into her mouth. Her head is tilted back in ecstasy as she chews noisily, grease running down her chin. She plucks out the heart and an eye, dropping them into her waiting mouth. Her eyes are twinkling "Those are the best parts!"

"I'm not eating that!" the other nurse snaps "I'm sorry, I just can't." She seems enraged. The remaining chicken is wandering around their feet. The plain nurse plucks it up and sets it in the microwave, on top of her sister's gore. Slams the door shut, sets the timer and the chicken begins to spin round and round.

The other nurse has left. I hear the plain nurse in another room, talking with someone female. I didn't hear this other person come in. I hope it isn't 'Pincurls'. If it is, I'm lost. They're smoking crystal meth. I can smell it. I know it might make them violent. I listen very carefully to monitor their mood. I want to be prepared in case they get crazy and try to kill me.

The second chicken is still turning in the microwave, it hasn't exploded yet. I can hear it giving out occasional worried clucks. There is smoke billowing out of the microwave now. The plain nurse rushes in and pokes at some of the buttons "It'll be okay, I'm not worried." she says in broken English as she returns to the other room and her friend.

Finally the chicken gives a muted PoP! The plain nurse hurries in, beaming at me as she passes. She's so excited about the whole thing, her eyes have a malevolent shine behind them. I think she might belong to some kind of cult.

The other woman wanders in. I'm horrified! It's 'Pincurls'. She stands there, staring at me, then she wanders into the kitchen. "I wonder where the boys got to?" asks the plain nurse to herself.

***

I'm back on the ward, in my bed. I was not killed after-all. The plain nurse is making her rounds as though nothing happened. I see the nurse who went off with 'the boys'. She talks with the plain nurse as though she hadn't done a thing wrong, and the plain nurse goes along with it! I think the plain nurse has low self-esteem.

She enters my room with a

beaming smile. I glare at her. I won't be nice to someone who abuses chickens, no matter how sorry I am for her. Besides, she did go along with the plan to kill me, whatever it was.

I think the plan was probably botched because the boys never came back. The problem is, she gave me a shot of something and I don't remember anything much after the second chicken explosion. All I have is a vague recollection of being bundled into a car. There's no telling what might have been done to me while I was out. I will not smile at her.

***

I'm gradually coming to figure out some things here. Often, at night, I have heard strange noises. Screaming of someone apparently being tortured in one of the rooms nearby. I hear tremendous splashes of water, and loud voices that I recognize as some of the nurses from this ward, and the crazy doctor.

At first, I thought there must be a swimming pool in one of the rooms, and that they were all playing in there. Maybe the screams came from them having fun? But often the screams sounded terrified. And the man making them was crying "Help! Stop it!"

One morning after the pool noises had been particularly rowdy the night before, one of the nurses commented to another "I guess the sixteen year olds were at it again last night!" She sounded almost proud of them. After hearing that, I figured there must be a special part of this ward for sixteen year old crazy people. Probably meth addicts. It was them who had been whooping it up in the pool.

I asked one of the nurses about the pool, but she looked at me like I was crazy "There's no pool here!"

Of course. Another thing for them to add to their list of things that don't exist, though I can see or hear them plainly. As soon as I said it, I worried that I should not have told her I suspected there was a pool. Now I know the splashing sounds I heard are top secret. I should not have let on that I know.

I know another thing too - there's more to this whole pool business. There's great danger there, not only for me, but for all the patents here.

***

Tonight I'm hearing a good deal more than ever before. We patients were all asleep, or nearly so, when I heard a sudden sound of several pairs of feet marching up the hall. I immediately realized it was Steve and the other two stooges. They were coming for me! My heart was pounding, I opened my mouth to scream. Then I had a horrible, selfish thought ... *'They might be after someone else! If I scream and draw attention to myself they might turn on me instead!'* And so I kept my silence in the hope that someone else was the target. Shame on me.

The target turned out to be the 'metal plate man'. I heard 'the three stooges' barge into his room. "Hey!" 'Metal plate man' cried in disbelief "I'm asleep! Leave me alone!" Then the sounds of 'the stooges' pulling him from his bed

105

and into his wheelchair. They roughly rolled him out the door and down the hall.

Now I hear his cries of fear. I hear the gruff voices of 'the stooges' and the crazy doctor and several of the nurses from the ward. I recognize especially the voice of 'Paris'. All of them ordering 'Metal plate man' to take off his clothes, then to get into the shower, then to drink something.

"Drink it all!" They demand, "Right Now!"

"I Can't!" he cries "I'm gonna be sick!" now I hear tremendous puking sounds and projectile diarrhea, a huge splash of water, and the staccato of tazers, more screaming, begging for help, begging for them to stop! After a while I hear the sound of him being wheeled in his wheelchair back to his bed. My door has been left half closed and I can't see much of anything out there.

So now I realize the nurse was telling the truth about one thing at least. There is no pool. The water sounded different this time - like it was being thrown from a bucket. I bet there are no sixteen year olds either. When the nurse made that comment about 'Sixteen year olds', she meant the nurses and doctor, and 'the stooges'. That means she and the other nurses are aware of what goes on, and they're just making jokes about it!

I'm wracking my brain to come up with an answer to this problem. What is the connection between the splashing, the drink, the tazer sounds, the vomiting and the diarrhea? What exactly were the doctor and nurses doing to the poor 'metal plate man'? And *why*?

It was obviously a punishment, but for *what*? Was he the victim the other times? No wonder he always seems so broken.

Every morning after an episode like last night, everyone acts like nothing happened. It's driving me crazy, seeing the faces of the very people who were attacking patients the night before. I have to pretend I know nothing about their secret lives. I have to let them inject me, and I have to swallow their medications and their food. I have to let them help me to the commode and wipe my butt. It would be dangerous to let on that I know so much. They would for sure kill me then.

For a while I was secretly tossing my medications under my bed after I realized these very pills would be the perfect way for them to poison me. The night janitor saw them there once as he was sweeping. It took a supreme effort not to look at him as I yelled at myself inside my head for getting caught. But he didn't turn me in. Instead he just grunted, then swept them up into his dust pan.

I was caught though, a few days later. A nurse saw me trying to casually flick my daily meds. under the bed and hurried to look. When she saw the small pile, she barked at me. I made a useless attempt at defending myself, but she would have none of it. Since then, I'm watched carefully as I take each and every pill.

***

They're at it again, second night in a row. It's the poor 'metal plate man' *again. His screams are so huge they're echoing down the* halls, into our rooms, melting into the walls.

I know that all the other patients on the ward are sitting up in their beds and listening. I can feel our combined sorrow and fear like porridge in the air. We're all being kept here like P.O.W.'s, listening to our fellow prisoner being tortured, knowing it will be any one of us next.

I listen carefully, trying not to let my horror and sympathy for 'Metal plate man' interfere with my investigation. I hear the splashing again, listen carefully ... it sounds like someone tossing a large pail full of water that hits 'Metal plate man' and then slaps against the floor. Immediately after, I hear the tazers, and 'Metal plate man' screaming. I believe I know what they're doing. They're wetting him down so the tazer will be more effective.

The drink is a mystery. It obviously causes the diarrhea and the vomiting, but what is it? And then it comes to me - it's the meth/gasoline drink I saw the orderly make! That's what is making 'metal plate man' so sick. I bet they gave him a 'meth enema' too.

I see 'Metal plate man' being wheeled back to his bed, past my room. His hair is wet and he's crying. I hear the nurses who participated in the crime, talking and laughing as they mop up the shit and puke. I sense the other patients sighing in resignation as they lay back on their pillows.

***

The plain nurse went with some of the others to the store for supplies this morning. Now she's back with a new pair of tight orthopedic socks for my swollen ankles. She thinks these will be less painful than the others. She's wrong, but I don't want to hurt her feelings. Despite my outrage at her for the chicken episode, I still like her and don't want her to be sad.

I hear the 'pretend orderly' moving up the hall with a trolley. Suddenly I hear the crazy doctor calling him to come into his office which is near my room. I can hear the crazy doctor yelling "I know you went to the store with those nurses! You were seen talking with a girl, and you went to her place and did drugs there!" 'Pretend orderly' protests, but the doctor doesn't believe him. He tells him to go back to his work.

'Pretend orderly' goes back to his trolley, but seconds later I hear the unmistakable sound of the 'three stooges' barging up the hall. I hear 'Pretend orderly' cry "No! Oh no, you've gotta be kidding!" They drag him back into the crazy doctor's office and slam the door shut. I hear 'Pretend orderly' shouting in pain as the 'stooges' beat him up.

He comes into my room when it's over. "Are you okay?!" I whisper to him. He flaps his hand, and with a rueful smile, tells me that he's fine.

***

Edward is here as a patient again. He's taken up with a group of patients from my room, who are all meth heads. There are four or five males including Ed, and one very thin, very slutty female. They've all left their beds and are living in the basement of the hospital. I can hear them down there, whooping and hollering. The whole ward can hear them, yet the staff just laughs it off. All the nurses are in love with Edward, especially 'Paris'.

He still visits me every day, wearing regular clothes. He's never in a hospital gown, ever. It's as though he doesn't want me to remember that he's a patient here just like me. I find it amazing that he can act so normal during these visits, even though he's loaded on meth and has been partying in that basement day and night for I don't know how long.

***

Last night I lay in bed, sleepily watching the nurses in their cafeteria across the hall. A hand-full of them were sitting at the table in their pajamas, enjoying some girl talk before bed. 'Paris' picked up her favorite theme, regaling them with fantastic tales about me. The other nurses hung onto every word for a while, but eventually they got up one by one, making a show of stretching and yawning as they made their excuses.

'Paris' blurted "Marian hates children." I could tell she was grasping at straws in the fear that she was losing her audience. "Especially Chinese children." She added.

The pregnant nurse gasped "So I guess I need to be especially careful around her then!" She and 'Paris' nodded gravely at each other.

"She kills them." 'Paris continued. "She told me she's

killed all of her own children."

I was gratified to hear several of them tell 'Paris' they thought this last story was a little over the top, as they shuffled off to bed. The pregnant nurse stayed on though, clearly upset at the news that I am a danger to her unborn child.

Later she came into my room, and asked if I have any children. I knew she was looking for guilt as she searched my face. I told her 'no', and saw her face fall. "But I love kids." I insisted. I felt like I was on trial. She'd already convicted me. She sees me as a child murderer now, there's nothing I can do about it.

***

This morning the nurses were all friendly with me. Feeling

better, after an uninterrupted night's sleep, I made a tiny joke with the Chinese nurse and she praised me for my sense of humor. "See? You *can* make jokes! You *can* smile!" she beamed.

The nurses are pretty much treating me like a slightly retarded child, but I'm loving it. Better that then having to fight them off. It's strange for me, seeing the same nurses who keep committing these outrages, now going about their nursing duties like nothing happened. But I know their secrets. I know how twisted they are behind closed doors.

Still, when I'm feeling as good as I am today, I smile and laugh with them. I'm not just *pretending* to be friendly with them, I'm finding I kind of *like* some of them. Not to mention, it can only be in my favor to befriend as many as I can. Next time there is a plan to kill me, these ones at least might not join the others.

Breakfast was good, and after breakfast, my medications and painkillers. Now I'm sitting up in bed, feeling a nice buzz, and combing my hair for the first time in a long time - maybe since I first came here.

Ed walks in, looking a little unsure. He beams when he sees me combing my hair. He looks so relieved. As though he had expected something completely off the wall from me. I don't understand, but I'll let it go. I'm having a wonderful day.

We have a nice visit, though I sense a sadness in him. I think about what he does when he's not visiting me. I'm confused about this ... how is it that he can stay in that basement day and night with those others, getting wasted, and then appear here beside my bed, perfectly groomed and insisting that he has never been a patient here? It's as though there are two Edwards. I wonder if the junkie Ed is not my Edward at all, but another patient? Or maybe he has developed a dual personality. I'll have to give this some thought.

***

'Paris's hatred for me has grown to huge proportions. I've heard her tell the other nurses that she's afraid of me. Of *me*! She won't even enter my room anymore, just glares at me every time she passes my door.

I heard her talking in the hall to some other nurses, all about how Ed and the other 'basement junkies' are planning some kind of attack on the head nurse.

'Paris' sounded very concerned about Edward. He might be hurt in the attack. I resented her for being concerned for *my* boyfriend as though she's personally involved with him. I started to feel worried about him as well, but then suddenly I felt nothing.

It was then I began to realize that I've lost him. He's become a different person and I don't like him this way. He lives in a whole different world now. I hear him and the others in the basement. It sounds like they're having the time of their lives. But why doesn't he invite me to join them? He obviously doesn't want me there. I think he doesn't even like me.

***

I'm standing behind some thick draperies pulled partway across to separate my small area from the main part of a huge room. In the middle of the room is a long, wooden table, and seated there is the head nurse, with her back to an open door leading outside. She's bent over a book.

I peek around the edge of the draperies to see through the open door - it opens level with the ground. It's dark outside. I've never been here before, and don't know why I'm here at all, but that seems to be the way these things always play out, so I'll just wait quietly to see what happens.

I remember the talk I heard between the nurses, about the rumor of an attack on the head nurse. I assume tonight is the night. I feel some concern for the nurse, but I'm also worried that I might be on the list for attack as well. With Ed changed so much, I don't know if he would hesitate to kill me if it should come to that. We are on opposite sides now, and he has an army while I stand alone.

I sense Edward and the 'basement junkies' moving around outside the door. The head nurse hasn't heard a thing. I realize I should warn her, but I'm not about to go against Edward, even though things are as they are. He might get hurt.

Ed and the others suddenly burst in, yelling and laughing like crazy people. All are wearing papier mache masks covering their entire head. The masks are giant - a dog, a horse, a bear ... all made up garishly with fur and what not.

In a terrifying rush, they pull the screaming head nurse from her chair and spray her full in the face with something from an aerosol can. Edward spots me and waves happily, his magnificent goat mask grinning with a mouth bigger than four of mine. At least he's not ashamed to acknowledge me in front of his friends. Maybe all is not lost after all.

***

Now the ward is abuzz with talk about the attack. The head nurse is in another hospital. I hear her entire face was eaten away by the stuff they sprayed on her. Also her leg was broken. Still, nobody has made any effort to evict Ed and the basement junkies from their lair.

Earlier today, Edward and his new friends came upstairs to my ward, with an offer of the masks they had made. They said they were a gift to be used to cheer up patients on the ward. The nurses were delighted. They arranged the giant masks all around the bed of a patient across the room from me.

That patient is in the same bed as the man with the dead animal gloves who has gone away. This new patient hasn't done any harm. He only lays there and pees all over his bed. He has a pair of rubber boots beside his bed and they are also filled with pee. The nurses have to pour them out. I wonder if that's why they put the masks around his bed - as a kind of charm to help him stop peeing all over.

I can't believe they've allowed those masks to stay. Don't they realize they're evil?! They have a kind of life of their own. They can hurt all of us! Besides, they look ridiculous taking up all the room around that poor peeing man's bed. The masks are each the size of one of those exercise balls. Each time the nurses try to attend to the peeing man, they have to clamber around the stupid things.

The nurses are terribly impressed with these masks. The fact that Ed and the 'basement junkies' are talented and conscientious enough to create these works of art (and that is what they are) has obviously cancelled out any ill feeling against them. They've become celebrities around here, even while the head nurse languishes in another hospital.

I'm hurt that Ed didn't invite me to help with the masks. He knows I know all about papier mache, I would have been an asset! Also I'm a little jealous because the masks are better than anything I've ever made.

***

The 'pretend orderly' comes in and stands by my bed. He makes a show of adjusting my intravenous bags, looking very nervous. Suddenly he drops a crumpled note onto my bed and rushes out of the room. I *knew* he was connected somehow with Ed and the 'basement junkies'! I think maybe they're all on my side and are going to try and rescue me!

Sure enough, the note is from Edward. There are instructions and diagrams of staircases and long hallways in some kind of theater. I'm to go to this theater tonight and wait for something, I don't know what.

It's night time, and I'm in the theater. Everything in here is dark and gloomy. I'm standing at the

126

top of a carpeted staircase, leaning against the railing, looking down on a stage with thick, velvet draperies. I've been here a long time and I'm thinking it was all a cruel hoax. But now I'm sensing someone behind me. A tall, male figure wearing a long, black robe, and a goat mask. I think it must be Edward. He leans close, and whispers in my ear "Go back to bed. This is not the time." He gives me a bear hug, and then he's gone.

Back in my bed, I look across at all the masks around the peeing man's bed. The goat mask is missing. Obviously Ed, or someone else snuck in here and retrieved that mask so it could be used in the meeting between Edward and me tonight, but why? What happened tonight, and what does it mean?

I believe something big is

taking place in the basement. Ed and his friends are planning something that will blow the lid off this place. I just wish he would include me. He wants to keep me separate from everything he's doing here. It makes me feel like such an outcast.

***

The crazy doctor has told me he intends to remove my catheter. "You don't even have to leave your bed!" he said "I can just do it right here!" He seemed quite excited.

Now he's sitting on the edge of my bed, drawing a diagram of my catheter. He draws a little balloon that is apparently attached to the tube inside me, and says he will give me a shot to deflate the balloon before he pulls the entire thing out. I'm afraid he's going to poison me, but I see no alternative. I'm so tired of fighting.

He injects me, and after a short time, slowly pulls out the catheter. I recognize the metal clamp that I saw on the other catheter I pulled out of myself. It's right before the now deflated balloon. No wonder I wasn't able to pull the other one out further! The balloon had still been inflated! Luckily I didn't injure myself! The catheter is completely out now. The doctor shows it to me and leaves with it. He'll probably use it in one of his sculptures.

***

Edward has decided to leave the basement and his new friends. I hear the nurses talking about it. He's come back up to the ward to get clean. I see him there in his bed across the room from me. It's the same bed that was used by the man with the dead animals, and the peeing man. The nurses removed all the masks, but they have left a tattered wily coyote doll hanging in the corner. I know it has the combined evil power of all the other masks. It's staring from its lofty position, down at Edward. Strangely, the wily coyote looks exactly like one I had years ago, including the dust and grime.

Now the basement junkies have come into the room. They all cheer when they see Ed, and jump onto his bed. They're lying on top of him and rolling around. He laughingly protests, then leans back against his pillow again. He looks very happy with his friends. He pays no attention to me. I pretend I don't care. The slutty girl lays back and invites Ed to make out with her. He gives a rueful grin and climbs on top of her.

I feel embarrassed because my entire family is here, seated on chairs and watching me being cheated on. I only just realized they're here. My mom and dad as well, even though they're dead. They look very much alive as they turn to gaze at me with expressions that say "How can you just let him do this to you?" I look back at them with a forced smile and tell them he's not really doing what it looks like he's doing. I'm beyond hurt. I'm so hurt I can't feel it anymore.

Ed and the basement junkies are all smoking meth now. So much for him getting clean. The nurses come in and order all except Edward to get out. One of them - a tall, shadowy man, hides under the bed and goes to sleep there. I whisper to the nurse that he's there, but she says it's okay. I worry that he'll try to kill me, but what can I do? I'll just stay awake all night again I guess.

**

I've noticed that the nurses are becoming more and more dependent on meth. They can't stop talking about how much fun they have on it.

"I want to do some right now!" squeals the pregnant nurse. "Let's make a drink!"

Her boyfriend comes in with another orderly. "We're making a drink!" The nurses cry out excitedly. They all rush into another room to prepare their concoction, the orderlies go to wait at the front desk. I can hear the nurses talking and laughing, advising the pregnant nurse as to the correct measurements for the drink.

At last they're ready. They call the two orderlies into the room. I hear the pregnant nurse asking to be first. I hear her drinking the stuff, and then I hear them giving her an enema. Shortly after I hear the sounds of diarrhea and vomiting. What exactly do they *get* out of this?! At least they're not pouring water and tazing themselves.

The rest of them take the 'cure'. The orderly who is the boyfriend of the pregnant nurse is complaining because the drink doesn't taste as it should. "You made it wrong!" he's accusing her "It's too weak!"

Suddenly, they're interrupted. A woman has come in off the street. She wants to be checked in.

133

She lists her ailments, but the staff don't think she needs to be admitted. Then the pregnant nurse has an idea. "Why don't you try this drink?" she suggests "It's fantastic! You'll feel much better!"

The woman agrees and I hear them all leading her away. I hear them telling her to take off her clothes and drink the meth concoction. I hear them giving her the enema. Again the diarrhea and vomiting. They don't wet or taze her. Amazingly, she keeps exclaiming how great it is, even as the shit and puke are spewing out of her!

She leaves, singing their praises. The pregnant nurse decides to make another batch. "This time," she tells the others "I'll do it really strong." When it's ready, she calls out to her boyfriend "I made it right this time!"

They're all about to go back into the room with their drink, when the woman off the street sails back in. "It felt so good, I want another one!" she declares. I'm disgusted with her. She's not even embarrassed about the enema! None of these people seem to mind debasing themselves in front of everyone!

The nurses and orderlies are hesitant - this batch was made much more potent than the first, but they relent, leading the woman back into the room.

The crazy doctor has joined them. He's making fun of the woman, though she doesn't seem to realize it. "I see you're very eager!" he chortles when he sees she has already taken off all of her clothes. I hear her swallow the drink, then lay down on the floor.

"I'm gonna give you a really Big one!" cries the crazy doctor as he shoves the enema in.

The woman starts puking and shitting again, but something is wrong. She's crying out "It doesn't taste the same as before! I want to stop!" But the nurses and orderlies keep yelling at her to lay still. The crazy doctor is shouting with glee as another ass load of diarrhea blasts out of her.

The orderlies and the crazy doctor have retreated to the front desk. The nurses are finishing with the woman from the street who is weeping now. Suddenly the woman lets out a horrific cry and falls silent. The crazy doctor calls from the front desk "Is she okay? What's going on in there?"

'Paris' opens the door a crack and answers in a sing song voice "She's dead."

136

The crazy doctor and the orderlies rush into the room, grabbing evidence in a frenzy. A new orderly who doesn't know the ropes here yet, has happened on the scene. He hurries to the phone at the front desk and calls for an ambulance. The crazy doctor barges up to him after he hangs up "Next time, give us a little more time before making that call." he mutters. The new orderly agrees, but he looks astonished and uncertain.

The crazy doctor goes back into the room and gives the dead woman another enema. "I have to do this to clean out most of the meth." he explains. "We don't want anyone finding anything during the autopsy."

I hear the nurses taking the dead woman out on a stretcher. "I hate it when they have white eyes." says 'Paris'. "When their eyes are open but not rolled up, that's okay. I just don't like the whites."

They set to work mopping up all the mess before the ambulance people get here. Everyone rushing around in a guilty panic. The ambulance people come quickly. They ask questions that the crazy doctor answers calmly. "The woman was probably an addict." he says "She probably overdosed."

***

It seems like it's been 'nearly Christmas' for ages. For a few days I was sure Christmas had come and gone, but today I learned that it's still over a week away.

I hear Carols being sung somewhere up the hall. The voices come slowly closer to my room.

It's the crazy doctor, the sock cutting doctor, and a bunch of the nurses, including 'Paris'. They all file slowly past, singing 'Hark the Harold Angels'.

I've moved down to the foot of my bed and am sitting cross-legged, watching and listening. It's so beautiful, I feel a lump in my throat. The crazy doctor turns and waves to me. I grin and wave back. I'm crying a little bit because it's all so beautiful. They move off but I can still hear them. Then they come back again, still singing. The crazy doctor turns to me and waves again. He urges the others to wave as well. Some of them do. I wave back, my eyes shining.

There are three nurses in my room. One of them tells me she asked them to wave especially to me. I can't get used to them changing so drastically from murderous crazy people to these kind, thoughtful care-givers. It catches me off guard every time. In a way, I have to hand it to 'Paris' who is, at least, honest in her feelings about me. She's playing games with me, but the 'let's pretend we didn't do anything crazy' game, she does not play.

***

The night shift has come in. 'Paris' among them. They're all in the little cafeteria room across the hall from me. I can see them and hear everything they say. They're very excited about something. "One of us always has to be on the ward." 'Paris' is instructing "We'll just take turns." The other nurses agree. Then they, all but one, begin to change from their nurses uniforms into sexy lingerie, chattering like school-girls.

They sashay down the hall together. I hear them enter one of the rooms. I hear a man's voice - it's the crazy doctor. The nurses are fussing over him as he splashes in water. I know now that there is a hot tub in there. They're all laughing at the crazy doctor's lewd jokes. He tells them what he wants them to do to him. I can hear it all.

One of the nurses is being ignored. I hear her complain "I guess nobody wants *me*." She leaves the hot tub and returns to the cafeteria to change back into her uniform. When she passes my room, I see that it is the Chinese nurse. Even though the crazy doctor is gross, I feel badly for her for being rejected.

She comes into my room to empty my commode. She smiles at

me, and I smile back. She takes the
commode bucket into the
bathroom - I know there's a sliding
glass door in the bathroom,
leading out to a narrow balcony.
The nurses leave the waste buckets
out there. I don't know why they
don't just flush them. When all the
buckets out on the balcony are full,
the nurses toss the waste over the
railing!

The nurses also have to take
turns making the food for us
patients. They're all quite proud of
their skills, each one making sure
to tell me I'm eating the
hamburger, or the meatless lasagna
that was made from scratch from
this treasured recipe or that one.
I'm concerned though, because I
saw 'Paris' frantically emptying
the fridge in the cafeteria the other
day. She'd discovered that half the
food in there was rotten.

***

I've been moved to another room. It's much bigger than the others, and there's just me. When they wheeled me in here, the drapes were open and the sun shining after several days of rain. I felt rejuvenated. The nurse hooked me up to the I.V., showed me how to use the remote and the phone, which are different in every room, and left.

This new room is right beside a room that the crazy doctor uses as an office. He has a computer in there and a printer. He's become interested in Edward's music after hearing that he writes, sings, and plays guitar.

Every day, he invites Ed to join him in that room, to go over the songs. Edward sings and sings while the crazy doctor records him. One time I heard the sock cutting doctor come in. He sat down to listen.

Ed went on for hours. The sock cutting doctor kept making noises about how he had things to do and must be going. Edward paid him no attention. "Wait! I have one more!" he said every time. Finally the doctor insisted on leaving and made his escape. As he passed my room I heard him muttering "*She's* okay, but *he's* nuts!" I felt happy at least that he thinks *I'm* alright. I can't afford to have both doctors hating me.

Now the crazy doctor has left Edward alone in his office. He's instructed Ed to keep recording himself. He will be in his other office having a meeting. He will have his intercom on so he and the other men at the meeting will be able to hear everything Edward records, and take notes as they listen. The crazy doctor is going to make the two of them famous!

Ed is in his element! The crazy doctor has all sorts of recording equipment in there. Also editing programs on his computer. I hear Edward singing his songs, ad-libbing funny sounds and jokes. I hear him mumbling to himself at the computer as he edits his work.

He's deleting a bunch of the doctor's stuff! And he's tearing up the doctor's papers! And he's getting louder! He's screaming into the microphone, imitating the cries I hear in the night when 'Metal plate man' is being tortured "Help! No! No! Stop! Please Stop!" He's making fun of him.

He's started calling me on my phone as well. I don't know how he got the number. The pregnant nurse is in my room folding laundry now. She heard my phone ring, and Edward talking to me on it even though I haven't picked up. Somehow his voice is coming through a loudspeaker for everyone to hear. His voice is animated. He's having fun. He calls me 'Twinkle' - his pet name for me.

I pick up the phone and hiss at him "Stop! Just Stop! This is not a good thing to be doing, you're going to get us both in trouble!" I sound like an old shrew, but I'm at the end of my rope. Ed sounds like a scolded child as he promises he won't phone me again. The nurse chooses not to get involved.

Now Edward has opened the door and is screaming out into the hall – Help! Stop It! You're Killing Me!" mimicking 'Metal plate man's' tortured screams. I guess he

thinks all of this will add some
unique element to the mixed tape
he's making. I can't *believe* he's
being so insensitive. 'Metal plate
man' has always been nice to him.
Surely he recognizes Edward's
voice, and knows he's being
ridiculed. I feel ashamed for Ed,
and for myself by association.

One of the nurses rushes up
and orders him to shut up. "Did the
doctor hear me?" he asks her
excitedly.

"Yes he did. Now please be
quiet." she tells him.

"Well? Did he like it?" he
persists.

"No! He hated it!" she lashes
out. I feel my heart breaking for
Edward. He must have truly
believed he was making a great
recording. I want to cry for him.

As he's pushed back inside
the room by the nurse, he keeps

repeating "I can't believe he didn't like it!" he sounds so crestfallen. This is a tragedy I don't want to hear.

The nurse discovers the torn paper all over the floor. She shouts at Ed, then leaves to get the crazy doctor. Edward is in deep trouble. He might be killed now. I wish I could get a message to him, but I'm tethered by my intravenous tube. Also, I feel strange about him. I don't know this Edward. I don't trust him. When he visits me, he's my Edward, but this other one … I don't know him.

The nurse has returned with the crazy doctor. The doctor shouts at Edward when he sees the mess. Ed had returned to his deleting of files and ripping of papers, and was in the middle of it when the doctor walked in. He grabs Edward and throws him across the room. Ed sounds totally surprised "Hey!" he cries "I was helping you! I thought we were partners!"

The crazy doctor calls for 'the three stooges'. My blood freezes. Now Edward will be beaten again, and I'll have to hear it all.

When 'the stooges' arrive, the doctor orders them to tie Ed up and lean him, sitting, against the wall. "And remove all of his white blood cells while you're at it!" he declares. "He'll be nothing but a red puddle on the floor by morning."

So now I'm keeping vigil over Edward again, powerless to do anything. 'The stooges' arrange him, tied, on the floor and run a small, hand-held machine, about the size of an electric shaver, over his body and face. There's a red light shining from it. It removes Ed's white blood cells.

149

After they leave, Edward asks the crazy doctor "So how come you didn't like my recording?" totally unconcerned that he's dying as he speaks.

"It was a huge disappointment!" the crazy doctor cries. "I expected excellence! What you gave me was amateur nonsense! What's with all that screaming anyway?!" The doctor is making fun of him now. Ed is silent.

I feel incredibly sad for him. Here he had been at the top of his game, creating a name for himself with his papier mache masks and his music. Now it's come to this miserable end. I do resent him. Still it's painful to witness his fall from grace.

The crazy doctor is trying to retrieve the files that were deleted. He swears at Ed over and over.

Finally he calls for 'the stooges' again. They barge in and the doctor cries "Take him to the shower! Get him out of here!"

I hear them dragging Ed out. He sounds weak, probably because he has no white blood cells. He's making a show of being brave. Singing and laughing at the top of his voice. 'The stooges' threaten him and order him to undress and get in the shower. I hear them turn on the water. Ed is splashing water all over, like a child in a bathtub.

Now I realize he *is* in a tub, not a shower. I hadn't realized they have bathtubs here. "Sit down in the swing!" one of 'the stooges' orders.

I understand now that there's a swing hanging from the ceiling, over the tub. It has a huge, white, plastic seat. It looks like something that would be in a

151

mental institution. The swing is raised or lowered with a series of pullies. The seat is like a big half bucket, with drain holes in the bottom. There's a bar that can be lowered in front of the patient, and locked with a padlock.

Ed gets into the swing and one of 'the stooges' lowers the bar and locks it. The swing is lowered into the water. Ed sings as he continues to splash. One of the 'stooges' is Black. Edward keeps calling him 'brotha' in a mocking voice.

'The stooges' are slapping him and pushing the shower nozzle in his mouth, turning on the water. They're trying to drown him! They alternately punch and wash him, punch and wash him. He continues to sing and make jokes. I don't know how he has so much energy with no white blood cells. I admire him for joking his way to his own demise instead of cringing. At the same time I'm horrified. "Stop!" I want to scream at him "Stop making everything worse for yourself and for me! I don't want to hear this!" But I keep silent in my bed, listening.

'The stooges' are tired and bored. They raise the swing, unlock and lift the bar and order Edward to come down. He refuses. They drag him out across the floor, beating and kicking him. Edward keeps laughing "Go ahead! I love it! You guys fags? Wanna suck my dick?" They put him back in the swing, lower the bar and lock it. They winch him down into the water again and turn on the tap. Then they leave.

I can hear the water flowing into the tub. The plug hasn't been pulled out. The water must be rising. The tub is deep and Edward is locked into the swing. But he appears not to care. He's still splashing and singing.

Finally he quiets. The water is still running. He might be drowned. I listen for sounds of life. Nothing. Dead again.

Towards morning, I hear a sudden gasp from Edward. He's still alive! The tap is still running and he's thrashing in the water. "Oh Shit it's cold!" he cries "Help! Help! The water's cold!" Finally someone comes in and turns off the tap. Edward is dried off and taken away. The hospital is without hot water now.

**

There's a lot of action in the crazy doctor's office next to my room. He's gotten the idea that this ward can create a reality show. I actually saw a commercial for it on TV. "New reality show coming your way this fall!" the announcer said "A hospital where anything can happen! There's even torture with drugs and tazers!" I've been hoping to see it again so I can point it out to Edward, and finally prove to him that all of this is actually happening, but so far no channel has played that commercial again.

The crazy doctor has all the nurses working overtime, scouring my journal and my poems for story lines, and printing them out. They have access to all my stuff now since the crazy doctor hacked into my computer. I see them taking turns at the computer in the staff room across from my room, often reading aloud. They exclaim and they whisper, putting forth theories on my present behavior as it relates to my personal history displayed before them in such intimate detail. They sit around a long table in the crazy doctor's office, reading their lines. I recognize all of it as my own writing.

They also practice singing Edward's songs. They plan to use them in the reality show. The doctor has them practicing so much it's interfering with their work. The other patients and I call for a nurse to come and help us with whatever we need, but there is no response. All the nurses are practicing for the show.

It seems like since all this reality show business started up, the crazy doctor and the chosen nurses have formed a kind of family. Those nurses who haven't been chosen for the show look on jealously as the lucky ones discuss their parts.

There's an older, disappointed looking nurse who strikes me as someone who always dreamed of being in the popular group but never succeeded. She hadn't been chosen to have a part in the show, and so she searched and searched through my writing on the computer, for a suitable role for herself. When she found it, she auditioned for the crazy doctor who grudgingly allowed her to join the cast. Now she prances around like twenty years have dropped off her age.

'Paris', the 'disappointed' nurse, and a chubby nurse who always snarls at all the patients, are getting ready for another night in the hot tub with the crazy doctor. The 'disappointed' nurse seems especially excited at the prospect. She's thrilled to be included. She

feels pretty. I can tell by the way she smiles at herself in the mirror. All three keep casting glances my way, giggling, as though they know something I don't know.

I soon find out what it is. I hear the women enter the room with the hot tub down the hall. I hear a male voice, but it's not the crazy doctor. It's Edward. He is waiting in the hot tub for them.

I hear 'Paris's' excited voice. This is her dream come true. Edward compliments them all and tells them to get in the hot tub with him. I hear them all splashing as they step inside. I hear them all making out. This is the end. I will not care about Edward anymore. We're finished. I feel like my insides are a frozen slab of meat. My grief is too much.

Now I'll feel really weird when Ed comes to visit. I feel

embarrassed, knowing the nurses know I'm being cheated on right under my nose. They're all laughing behind my back.

***

All the staff had been talking for days about the possibility that the Norol virus might get into the hospital. Now they tell me I'm the first one on my ward to have it, and I'm contagious. They have orders to not come into my room unless they have a mask over their mouth and nose, also a special gown, gloves and booties. They've put a garbage can by the door so they can strip everything off and dump it in there before they leave my room. They tell Edward he must do the same when he visits me. I hear them warning other patients' visitors to come onto this ward at their own risk.

I know the truth. I don't have Norol virus at all. I am actually suffering from the effects of the latest attempt on my life.

The other night a group of nurses swept into my room and injected me before I could stop them. They stood in a group around my bed as I began to slip away. 'Pincurls' was among them. She leaned close and whispered to me that I'd just been given an overdose of the meth concoction. She looked victorious. I realized I had lost the war. I was dying. But somehow I didn't care anymore. It was too late now, I might as well relax. It wasn't so bad after all, to be killed. "Ah, she's going now." One of the nurses whispered as I slipped peacefully away.

I didn't die. I woke up the following morning and suddenly

felt vomit roaring up my throat. As I puked my insides out, the acrid smell of burning chemicals rose in a spiral that I actually saw, like a cartoon, from the top of my head. I understood then that a small circle of my skull was actually burning. "She's got Norol virus." One of the nurses declared, and that was that. Case closed.

***

Edward has been asked to join the crazy doctor and the chosen nurses in their practice for the reality show. He and the crazy doctor are pals once more. The nurses are all giddy about spending more time with Edward. Especially 'Paris'.

The nurses have been whispering about something concerning Edward all afternoon.

Apparently he's planning on escaping from here. All day he's been holed up in the crazy doctor's office beside my room. He's allowed in there again. Because he's on the reality show. He's the hospital Golden Boy. He can get away with anything and he knows it.

I hear him in there, scrolling through the notes the crazy doctor has on his computer. Notes about the reality show - which of my poems and stories will be used and who will act out which part. Ed is reading rapidly to himself, scrutinizing the lines for evidence against himself or me which he then deletes. He's also changed some of the lines. He's making sure they can't find out that I'm an illegal alien. I feel a sad sort of happiness in the fact that he's still thinking of me.

Now I hear him reading aloud about alarm systems. I think he's planning the escape tonight! I'm worried about him getting hurt. What will he do when he's out in the streets anyway? He won't have any clothes or shoes. He won't have his keys or wallet. He'll be wanted by the police.

I'm tense every time I hear footsteps coming down the hall. I worry that the crazy doctor or a nurse who doesn't care for Ed the way the others do, will walk in on him and catch him. I can't warn him because that would draw attention to what he's doing. All I can do is sit here in bed, straining my ears to hear what will happen.

Now it's late in the night. I hear Ed rummaging around. Now he's started the shower. I can't believe he's wasting time taking a shower when he needs to be going!

What is *wrong* with him?! Even though I don't want him to risk escaping, I feel impatient with him for being so casual and slow.

But now I remember that this is all part of the plan. In order to foil the alarms he must be completely wet, especially his feet. Next he must tiptoe down the hall to the first alarm light that is mounted high up on the wall. For five minutes he must stand there in the puddle that forms around his feet, then hurry to the next light. In this way he will not trip the alarm.

I also remember that I've been given instructions. I'm to fill a plastic bag with clothes for him, and leave it for him just inside my open door. I can't leave my bed because I'm attached by the intravenous tube, but I manage to fling the bag so that it slides up just to the right spot. I also know now that Edward wants me to come with him if I choose. He'll come to me before he leaves, I'll give him my answer then.

I hear him now, easing the door of the office open and creeping up the hall to my room. He's going through with it. I can only hope he survives. He's come into my room and is standing beside my bed. He seems different. This is Edward's alter personality - in a way it's not really him at all. I've decided I won't go with him.

"I understand." he whispers. He hands me a plastic bag with clothes for me. "In case you change your mind." he says. "If you decide to come, make sure you don't step on this carpet beside your bed. It's alarmed. You have to step on the commode, then jump over to that chair over there. Do you think you can do it?"

I shake my arm, attached as it is to the intravenous drip "I'm not brave enough to go." I tell him. "Besides, I don't know how to get this intravenous tube out." He kisses me on the forehead and leaves. Like a ghost in the night, he's gone.

I hear him stopping under the first alarm light. I count out the minutes. I hear him move to the second light and begin to count again. Now there's a shout! A nurse has seen him and pulled the alarm. Its shrieks echo through the hospital. Edward has slipped into a room and is hiding.

I hear the police now, pounding up and down the halls on every floor. Their noise is tremendous, along with the alarm that no one has thought to turn off. The police are all armed to the teeth. They have dogs.

They've found several of
Ed's puddles. Noticing that every
puddle is directly across from an
alarm light, they hold a conference
there in the hall. One of them
recalls the practice of wetting
one's self down to avoid setting off
an alarm. The policemen decide
that they too must wet themselves
down and stand for five minutes at
every alarm light. In this way, they
will be sure to catch Edward. I'm
not sure how this works, but they
seem convinced.

All of this showering and
standing for five minutes is eating
into their time. They keep
complaining as they are forced to
stand shivering "He's probably
miles from here by now!"

I know that Ed is nearly free.
I know also that the front door is
locked. The only way to unlock it
is to purposely set off the final

alarm and then run through the door before anyone can catch him. He'll have only a few seconds. He's crouched under the front desk now, waiting for his moment.

The crazy doctor has come blustering on the scene. He can't believe there's been an escape on his watch. He's worried about losing his job. "We need to evacuate all the children!" he cries. Then he gathers up all the chosen nurses and orders them to stand in a group and sing the songs they've practiced so hard to learn. After a while they also sing Christmas carols. Somehow this bedlam is all meant to calm any visitors that might be here, so they won't think this hospital is badly run.

Now I hear the front door alarm. Edward has activated it to unlock the door. It's now or never.

I hear his desperate dash across the floor. The cops are galloping as a herd toward him, slipping in the water, cursing and bellowing. The crazy doctor is madly conducting the nurses as they sing louder and gayer than before.

And then they stop singing. Edward has gotten away. The police and the dogs are chasing him somewhere out there in the night. The crazy doctor orders that everyone on the ward should gather in the nurse's cafeteria for our own safety. I hear the nurses moving from room to room, wheeling the patients down the hall to the cafeteria. No one comes to my room. They've forgotten me.

I'm not sure what the danger is for me, but I'm afraid. What if there's a shootout and I'm trapped here attached by my intravenous tube while the rest are safely behind the cafeteria door? I call out to every nurse who passes by "Please help me, I can't get out of bed!" They just tell me to wait. Then they tell me they can't detach the intravenous tube until the doctor okay's it. I call out to the doctor when I see him, but he's distracted by the escape and ignores me.

One of the nurses asks me why I want to get out of bed. I tell her 'because we're all supposed to go to the cafeteria so we're safe!' I can't believe she asked me such a stupid question. She tells me "Nobody's going to the cafeteria."

"But isn't it dangerous out here?" I ask her. Amazingly, she looks at me like I'm crazy. She seems quite unfazed about all that has gone on tonight.

Now I hear the nurses talking

about stripping all the beds and then moving every patient to a different room. Somehow, all of this is meant as a safety precaution. They peek around my door into my room. "I'm surprised he didn't take her with him." whispers 'Paris'. She sounds like she's gloating.

One of the other nurses comes to my rescue "He probably wanted to spare her life." she says, wisely. The rest all nod in agreement. 'Paris' looks jealous.

The kind nurse indicates the plastic bag with clothes that I had tossed toward my open door for Edward. He decided against taking it with him. "So she *was* aware of his plan then." she says, adding that several of the other patients also had these plastic, clothes filled bags tossed near their open doors. From the list of names she recites, I recognize that these are the former 'basement junkies' who have since all returned from the basement to their beds.

"She's just sitting there in her bed!" 'Paris' fumes, meaning me. "She never helps out around here! She just sleeps and expects to be waited on hand and foot!" They all move off to various rooms to strip the beds.

I hear some of them in the crazy doctor's office. They're reading aloud a note that Ed left on the computer. In it, he lists several names. I recognize them again, as the 'basement junkies'. Apparently he's planning to meet up with them on the outside. My name is mentioned as well. The instructions are for me to contact as many of the 'basement junkies' as I can, here in the hospital. I'm quite excited by all of this. I'm finally being included in Edward's plans.

Now I'm being scolded again. After I heard 'Paris' complaining about my not helping out, I decided to strip my own bed. I wasn't able to move around very well because of the intravenous tubes, but by leaning across the bed, I managed to pull off all the bedding and dump it on the floor. Now two nurses have come in, seen the pile of blankets and sheets, and they're annoyed with me. I don't get it. They complain about my not helping, then complain about my helping. I can't win.

I explain why I did it "I was trying to be helpful." I insist. "I heard some nurses saying I never help out, and I decided to try and do what I could, especially now since you have all this commotion because of the escape."

One nurse catches the eye of the other one. "That was very nice of you." she tells me carefully, like I'm the crazy one. Like I'm slightly dangerous. "Wasn't that nice of Marian to help out." she asks the other nurse, who nods slowly.

The police have come back now. They didn't find Edward. He actually pulled it off. I hear the police talking to the crazy doctor. The doctor tells them where they can post snipers along the roof. I know that Ed is far away. He'll keep to the back roads, and travel only at night. He'll live a hard and dangerous life as a fugitive. I wonder if I'll ever see him again.

**

The other day I noticed a plastic Safeway bag among my

own bags on the windowsill. The nurses placed my things there when they moved me to this room. I looked in the bag and found several packages of raw bacon inside. I alerted a nurse when she came in, stressing that the bacon did not belong to me. She peered doubtfully into the bag and then left without it. It's there still, moldering in the sun. I'm sure they'll blame me when it starts to stink.

The nurses have come to take me to a new room. They fuss around with the metal coat rack that holds all the intravenous bags that are apparently keeping me alive. There's also a computer-like box on another pole that blips out something about me when the nurses press the buttons. All of this must be gathered up, and me, lying in state on my bed, wheeled down the corridor to my new accommodations. It's all quite exciting. I look around as we pass each room. I haven't been out in the hall for so long, I have no idea of the layout. It's very strange to see for myself what my surroundings look like.

Before we left my room, the nurses gathered up my bags of belongings that were on the window sill. I remembered the Safeway bag of bacon. "That's not mine." I told them several times, but they ignored me. I couldn't let them go on thinking it was mine. I kept repeating "That's not mine. It must have been left here by the last patient. Please throw it away." They wouldn't listen.

Now I see they've taken it, along with my belongings, to my new room. It's been placed beside my bed. Why in the world would these supposedly trained nurses insist on keeping this raw meat? There must be some ulterior motive that I'm not seeing.

My new room is much smaller than the big room I just came from. And there are two other beds in here. 'Paris' muttered to the other nurses after they settled me in "I chose that big room for her myself, just to be nice. I thought she'd appreciate it but no! She didn't stop causing trouble the whole time she was in that room!" I have no idea what she's talking about.

"She's a slut!" 'Paris' declared to everyone who would listen, "I've seen pictures of her online. She posed naked for those *disgusting* pictures. She sleeps with her legs outside the blanket too, hoping for a man to walk by and see her!"

Now a janitor has come in. I indicate the bag of bacon "That's not mine." I tell him. I don't want him to think I'm the kind of person who would keep raw meat out like that. But when I ask him to throw it away, he tells me he's not authorized to do it.

***

It's several days since Edward's daring escape. Now everyone is running around all excited. He has been recaptured. I've left my bed and am standing in the hall with the nurses, watching as Edward is pushed into a room, followed by the crazy doctor and the 'three stooges'. He's going to be beaten, maybe worse.

"I'm just heart broken." mutters 'Paris' "Oh, I'm just

broken hearted." She's acting as though she's his girlfriend. I'm just a by-stander here as far as 'Paris' is concerned. Edward is pretending he's not afraid, cracking jokes and laughing. I turn to one of the nurses,

"He's not like this normally." I beg her to believe me "He shouldn't be punished, he's sick, this is not the real him!"

***

Ed's beating has been administered, now he's in a bath tub, recuperating. 'Paris' and three other nurses have been summoned to his room. They're all wearing lingerie again.

"Look at my balls!" he rages "Look at them!" The nurses gasp. The 'three stooges' have mangled Edward's testicles so badly, they don't look real. Even 'Paris' doesn't want to get near them. "Go get that blond nurse then!" Edward demands, "She'll suck my dick for me. The rest of you are all cunts."

The blond nurse is summoned. She enters the room and immediately takes charge. Stepping into the tub with Edward, she gives him a blowjob, then applies some salve to his balls. He then orders her to leave. "I just want to sleep." he mumbles "You're all cunts. Fuck off."

***

A new, young nurse has started working here. She seems very kind. The night janitor and I talked with her yesterday as she was fiddling with my intravenous tubes. She told us about her life and how she's working hard to make something of herself, even though she's just twenty-one. We both admired her and told her she was smart.

She's been told to be careful around me. "She kicks." One of the other nurses told her when she was first introduced to me. As I talked with her and the night janitor, I noticed her eyeing my feet every time I re-crossed my legs under the blankets.

I wanted to tell her that I'm smart too. I've accomplished things. I wanted to tell her that I would never kick anyone who wasn't trying to kill me, but I didn't have the words, somehow. And if I could have found them, I understood that it wouldn't mean anything to the young nurse. I've become nothing more than a patient. A lost and crazy patient who probably won't make it out of the asylum.

***

Three of the nurses came into my room tonight. One of them wakened the woman in the bed next to mine; the only other patient in the room besides me. The nurse whispered to her "I'm just going to have you wait outside the hospital for a little while." as she bundled the mildly protesting patient into a wheelchair. "It's a 'black coat' night." she told the woman, by way of explanation. "You won't have to be out there too long." I realized that they were taking her out of here so she wouldn't be a witness to whatever they planned to do to me.

After the patient had been wheeled out, the nurses took me from my bed and, each holding me up under one arm, ushered me down the hall to a staircase I hadn't known was there before. We went down to the basement. The nurses told me I was expected to pose for the doctor's camera. After that, I would be given the meth concoction, and tazed.

The three nurses have been joined by several others, including the new, young nurse who was talking with me and the janitor. They're all sitting at the other end of the room, talking about nothing. We're all waiting for the doctor to be finished with Edward, who is in a small adjoining room with him, being tortured in the usual way.

I'm trying not to cringe at his screams. I won't let them know that their actions are having any effect on me at all. The doctor comes out and points at me. "You're next!" he barks, then he returns to the room where Edward is waiting to be tortured some more. I continue to pretend I feel nothing.

The nurses are growing bored. They're not paying any attention to me since I'm just lying here. Every once in a while, they mention to each other how strange it is that I don't seem to be affected by Edward's cries. They call me 'cold'. They will not recognize that I've been terrified into doing nothing at all. But I'm screaming now. As loud as I can. Also I've remembered my phone. I call 911 again. The police are on their way.

The new, young nurse comes to crouch beside my bed. "You're in a hospital." she croons "We're trying to help you." Why do they always say exactly the same thing when trying to reassure me? They always say it in an absurdly calm voice, their expression carefully blank. I find it terrifying, especially since they're saying it while trying to kill me.

"Why are you doing this?!" my voice is pitiful. "I have to be here, but you can go, you don't have to be like them." I indicate the other nurses. Maybe I can save her from becoming a lunatic like the rest. It will be my good deed. Also, if I convince her to leave the basement, that's one less person I have to fight off. "You're too smart for this." I tell her. She asks me to repeat what I said. I do. She gets up and holds a whispered conversation with another nurse. Together they walk out of the room. I've succeeded in getting through to her at least.

Now the police are here. I hear them roaring up into the parking lot. Here in the basement,

185

the nurses have been joined by several of the orderlies. They all have their tazers ready.

I notice now that the pregnant nurse has brought her water-head baby in here. He's in his carrier on the table beside my bed. Apparently he will be included in the photos of me. I'm going to be involved in child pornography now. I hear that 'Pincurls' is the one who set it up.

The police have sent a female cop to knock on the basement door. The door is right across from my bed. The nurses let her come right inside. There's something not quite right going on here. The cop doesn't seem fazed to see me, waiting my turn to be tortured and photographed with this poor disabled baby.

She's standing near my bed, talking to the baby's mother as

though they're friends. "I don't mind what else you do," she tells her, "but I can't condone using a child for pornography. That I can't allow." Everyone nods in agreement, including the pregnant nurse who doesn't seem at all embarrassed that she was called out for trying to use her child in pornography. She offers the cop some meth, and the cop suddenly drops all pretense of being professional. Now she's just another junkie, scoring drugs. She leaves with a little baggie of stuff without any further mention of the baby, or me, or Ed in the next room.

An hour or so has passed. The orderlies are all arranged at the windows which they have slid open so they can shoot their tazers. One of them lets off an occasional blast. The cops fire back, but there is no passion, everyone is getting tired of it. Now the police have put down their guns and are just throwing rocks at the hospital.

The orderlies have all left. Ed and the doctor are quiet in the other room. The nurses are entertaining themselves by fiddling with the camera equipment that is to be used in the photo shoot. "I'm bored." says one. "Maybe it's not going to happen tonight after all."

***

I've been told that I can go home tomorrow, but I've heard this before. Still, I'm optimistic because I've been moved to another building called 'the nurse's quarters'. At no other time, when they told me I would be going home, have they taken this step. I think it might be real this time after all!

I had no idea the nurses all lived together in this dorm-like place. Apparently all the patients who are released from the hospital spend their final night here as a sort of half-way house to ease their transition into the outside world.

I'm a little nervous because I suspect that none of the previously discharged patients actually made it home. I have a frightening theory that they are actually taken out and killed. Hopefully Edward will get here before anything like that happens.

I also know that they always take a 'going home' picture with each beaming patient together with the doctors and nurses. I discovered this when I heard other patients being released and having their picture taken, out by the front desk. I heard all the staff cheering because the patient was healed and could now graduate to the outside world.

I won't be having my picture taken though. I overheard the crazy doctor exclaiming when he heard I was to be released "She can go I guess, if there's no further way to keep her here. But she's not getting the royal treatment! She's caused us enough trouble, she doesn't deserve it!" He's furious that he never got to have his way with me. He feels like something has been stolen from him and he blames me for it. "The next one is Mine!" he roared as he stomped up the hall.

***

The setup here in the nurse's quarters is the same as my ward.

There's even a nurses cafeteria across the hall, just like at the hospital. It's evening now. My final night, if all goes well.

'Paris' and the 'disappointed' nurse are in the cafeteria, hurrying into their lingerie. The crazy doctor has declared another hot tub party. The hot tub is on the floor below, accessed by a staircase leading from the cafeteria. The doctor is in there now with the 'pretend orderly'. I can hear them splashing around. 'Pretend orderly' laughs at all the crazy doctor's lame jokes, making a show of it, as though he's having a wonderful time. I realize he has no choice but to be part of this, still I can't help but feel a little bit contemptuous. He seems to be playing the part without any difficulty at all.

'Paris' exudes confidence as she fusses in front of the mirror.

'Disappointed nurse' is less pleased with herself. Her lingerie is totally out of style. She looks ridiculous and I suspect she knows it.

"You look great!" 'Paris' tells her. Amazingly, this is all the other nurse needs to hear. Now she's smiling smugly at her reflection. She can't wait to get started. But the doctor is shouting again from the hot tub room. He wants the two nurses to go to the store and bring back a feast. The two women immediately change into street clothes and scurry out the door.

When they return, they have several bags of takeout food. It smells delicious. They bustle around, arranging the food on a tray, careful to make everything perfect, then they change again into lingerie, retouch their makeup, whisk up the food tray, and clatter down the stairs in their high heels to the hot tub where the men are waiting.

They're both giggling and flushed. 'Paris' is in her element, but I sense that the other nurse feels out of her depth. She darted me a hateful, victorious look as they passed my door. She thinks she's won by being chosen for this, and she's laughing at me for not being part of the group, for being an outsider as she has spent her life being. These types are the most dangerous because they have a lot to prove, or disprove as the case may be.

I hear them enter the hot tub room. They set the food laden tray down on the floor and stand there, awaiting instructions. But the crazy doctor is angry. He shouts at them and orders the 'disappointed' nurse to take the tray away,

193

rearrange the food, and return with it. "Quick!" he explodes.

The 'disappointed' nurse is crying as she hurries back up to the cafeteria with the tray. "It's my fault." she mutters to herself as she moves the food around, trying to find the ideal arrangement to please the crazy doctor "I didn't do it right. It's my fault. My fault. My fault." Then she rushes back with the tray, pathetically hopeful that she's done something right in this situation that is so beyond her scope.

The doctor is yelling at her again. I can't make out all the words. He orders her to leave. She stumbles back up the stairs, weeping. Now she's on the phone, pouring out her sorrows to a friend on the other end of the line. "I got fired." she stammers "I can't believe it, I'm out of a job."

'Paris' enters the room with the tray. The food is untouched. Together the two rejected nurses wrap up the food and put it away. They're quiet now. Embarrassed. All their earlier excitement has vanished. But when the crazy doctor suddenly calls them back, they leap to attention. All smiles as they clatter back to the hot tub room, the crazy doctor, and the 'pretend orderly'.

All is quiet now, except for the muted sounds I hear from the hot tub room. I guess all the other nurses are working at the hospital. I seem to be alone. I try to relax in my bed, watching t.v., hoping the crazy doctor doesn't take it into his mind to include me in their little party.

Suddenly he yells up at me to change the channel. "You know which one I like!"

I have no idea which channel he wants, and suddenly I can't seem to work the remote control. The crazy doctor and the 'pretend orderly' are laughing at me, taking turns yelling non-sensical orders. "Channel 6!" they cry out jubilantly. I try it, and they yell out another number "That's not the right channel! Try channel 8!" I realize that 'Pretend orderly' is only doing what he has to do in order to survive, but I hate him now for playing along with such obvious enthusiasm.

I've been desperately switching channels for ages now. I'm crying in frustration. This remote control seems to be broken. I try using the phone - it looks very much like the remote, I'm wondering if I got the two mixed up in my frightened confusion. I aim the phone at the t.v. and press some of the buttons. Nothing. I try the remote again, *why* is the stupid thing not working?!

Finally I call out "I don't know how to find the right channel! Please tell me how to do it!" I'm so frustrated, I'm trembling. I'm afraid that if I don't get the correct channel, the doctor will hurt me or even kill me. The two men just laugh and call out some more numbers. "Will someone please come and help me with this!"

"Why don't you try number 6, and then number 8?" comes the sudden, unexpected voice of the 'disappointed' nurse. She's come up from the hot tub room for a moment, all smiles now that she's been given her job back after all. I tell her I already tried that a dozen times, but she's gone back to ignoring me and is heading back to the party. The crazy doctor yells again, he and 'Pretend orderly' laugh together.

My phone rings. It's Edward. I tell him urgently about my predicament, but he reacts as though I'm making a mistake somehow. "No doctor would ever make a patient switch the channel for him!" he exclaims "They're way too busy for shit like that! Just don't worry about it!" I don't tell him that the "busy doctor" is, at this moment, in the hot tub with another guy and two nurses. He wouldn't believe me anyway.

I struggle desperately to explain my fear of the doctor, but Ed doesn't understand. "Just watch whatever you want." he says impatiently. But now the crazy doctor is yelling at me again. I can't listen to both him and Edward at once. I need to pay full attention to the most dangerous one. I hang up on Edward. I don't know what else to do.

All four in the hot tub yell together, shouting and laughing "You have to press 6, then 8, then 10, then 6 again, then 5!" I stab at the numbers, getting the order wrong, weeping in frustration as I call out for them to repeat it. They do several times, getting more and more boisterous. I can't make out what they're saying.

"There's a dead cat on the stairs I'll have to step over if I come up there!" shouts "Pretend orderly". Finally they fall silent. In the quiet, the crazy doctor exclaims "Gawd she's stupid!"

The doctor and "Pretend orderly" are still in the hot tub, though 'Paris' and the 'disappointed' nurse have left. I hear the two men talking about me.

"That chick's nuts!" exclaims the doctor. 'Pretend orderly' agrees with a chuckle and calls out half-heartedly for me to switch the channel again. I ignore them now. I've turned off my t.v.

It's relatively quiet now. They've lost interest in me. I'm feeling more relaxed. I phone Edward, trying several times because I can never remember the number. When he picks up, I laugh with relief "It's okay now. It's okay now."

***

The nurse's quarters were noisy last night, with all the nurses coming off shift. They all seated themselves at a long table, tiredly finishing their supper before heading off to bed.

After a good night's sleep, I awake

at dawn. I'm excited about leaving today, but cautious. I don't want to raise my hopes too much in case they should, once again, decide that I need to remain in the hospital.

The Chinese nurse is in charge here at the nurse's quarters. She goes to several of the beds where the other nurses are sleeping, and wakes them up. "Time for your shower." she whispers. She seems to be waking them in shifts. When one group is out of the shower, they settle down at the long table in the cafeteria for breakfast while another group showers. Finally they're all ready to go to work.

As the nurses were readying for their day, I tried several times to get out of bed, but each time, the Chinese nurse ordered me back. "I need to get ready." I kept trying to explain, but she would have none of it. I'd planned to go shopping today. I was looking forward to having a nice, normal day. But the Chinese nurse tells me I need to be quiet and go back to sleep. "But it's my last day!" I kept begging her.

"Well there's another good reason to stay in bed!" she cried out cheerily each time "You get to just relax and take it easy!" Briskly she would push me back down on the bed and pull the covers up to my chin. My worst fears are coming true once again - the nurses are planning something new to keep me in this place. I've written down Edward's phone number on several pieces of paper and hidden them in different places, including inside my socks between my toes. At all cost, I can't let anyone find them or I'll lose my only connection to safety.

I'm back on the ward again, in my room. I'm sitting up in bed, anxiously waiting for news of when I can go home. I don't know how I got back here from the nurses quarters. I assume the Chinese nurse drove me. Every time a nurse passes my door, I call out to her "When can I go home?" The answer is always the same. I need to wait for the doctor to speak with me. I need to speak with a psychiatrist. I need to have a place to go, a ride, and a goal for my new non-drinking life. 'Would I consider A.A.?' they ask again and again.

The 'sock cutting' doctor comes into my room and stands gazing at me from the foot of my bed. I ask if I can go home and he tells me "Maybe tomorrow."

I can't believe it. They've

done it again. I beg him to no avail. He keeps shaking his head "We need to be certain you're well enough to leave here." I can't tell him I won't be well *until* I leave, because he'll think I'm crazy if I start going on again about staff trying to kill me. I have to maintain a perfect facade of calm and good health. But it's no good. I'm not going home today after all.

***

Since my latest almost release from here, my senses have been on high alert. I know the crazy doctor is feeling pressure to make his move on me soon, before I get discharged and leave his clutches forever. This latest was too close for his liking.

And sure enough, it's happening tonight. I've been

sensing something all day from the nurses. Now it's evening, visiting hours are over, the ward is quiet. I hear them talking outside my door, arguing over who should "do it" and where. Then "Pincurls" shows up. This is it.

"You're the only one who can do it!" they all clamour around her "You're the one for the job!"

'Pincurls' is obviously pleased to hear all of this, and begins, as she has many times before, to list the ways she would like to hurt me. "I'd stab her." She says "But I'd beat the shit out of her first."

"Take her outside!" one of the other nurses interrupts, "We'll tell her you're taking her for a walk, that it's a treat!" They all murmur and nod, but I sense an undertone of hesitation in the nurses, including 'Pincurls' - like they're not even close to being as tough as they're pretending. Still, scared bullies can be as dangerous as anyone else. I don't feel safe just because they're nervous about killing me. Still it's good to know.

The plan is set. In half an hour, 'Pincurls' will come to my bed and tell me I'm to go for a walk with her. Then she will beat me up, and stab me to death. I'm sitting up, pretending to watch t.v., glaring at any nurse who walks, smiling, into my room. "Are you up for a little walk tonight?" several of them have asked me brightly. Five minutes left. And then the sky opens and it's a thunderous downpour outside. 'Pincurls' immediately calls the whole thing off. The nurses agree. But I should be moved to another room, they decide, where I'll be alone.

***

I spent one night with an empty bed on either side of my own. Now they've brought another patient in. As the nurses push her past my bed, she blurts "I hate her!", nodding her head in my direction "I want my curtain all the way closed so I don't have to look at her!" I'm glad she was dumb enough to show her colours right away. Now at least I know whose side she's on. She'll probably try to kill me too.

Every room here has a computer in it. They're for the staff, we patients are not allowed to touch them. My new room-mate has tiptoed from her bed and is frantically clicking away at the keyboard. Now she's got a friend on the phone, she's making plans to escape. She's packing her bag with one hand, typing with the other, her phone pinched between her ear and her shoulder, barking orders to her friend who is to be here in a getaway car. And then she's caught. A nurse pulls her away from the computer and tucks her back into bed.

***

The night staff have come on shift. I'm pretending to sleep. The orderly who goes out with the pregnant nurse comes in and sits on a chair under the window. When I open my eyes, he tells me he has been ordered to watch me. I pretend to sleep. I hear a group of nurses walking down the hall, calling out gaily that it's nice to have some time off. They're all leaving the hospital! Something is about to happen.

'Pincurls' saunters in, right up to the orderly, who gathers her into his lap. They start making out, after only a mild protest from 'Pincurls'.

After a while, she gets up and I hear her talking under her breath to the woman in the bed next to mine. "Whatever happens tonight, you didn't hear anything. Understand?" She has to repeat herself several times until the woman acknowledges that she has heard.

The orderly, still sitting in his chair, mutters at 'Pincurls' to 'take her outside'. 'Pincurls' helps the woman into a wheelchair and out the door. I continue to pretend to be sleeping. My heart is hammering, everything feels very precarious.

'Pincurls' has been making

out with the orderly for some time. I slit my eyes open only occasionally, and very carefully, to keep from being discovered awake. Now she's approaching my bed. She leans over my shoulder from behind, her breath close to my ear. She's tickling my ear with a feather. I think she wants to have a threesome with myself and the orderly. "I'm not interested." I tell her firmly. "What you do with him is none of my business, but I'm not interested. I just want to sleep."

After a while, she approaches me again, this time with a needle. I must not allow her, of all people, to inject me. I don't believe she's really a nurse. I yell and struggle until she gives up. "I'm going to get help." She whispers to the orderly who is still seated in his chair, watching without much interest.

As soon as 'Pincurls' leaves the room, I ease out from under the covers. My feet touch the floor. I take a step towards the door. I can't believe I'm falling. I'm on my back on the floor, my legs sticking straight up like a cartoon. I'm laughing because I look like a cartoon. I can't believe I'm laughing. The orderly helps me back into bed.

I'm gazing down at my arm as 'Pincurls' tries to jab the needle in. I've stopped fighting because I've discovered something fascinating - 'Pincurls' doesn't seem to know how to inject me. She's unable to do it. She couldn't even wind the tourniquet around my upper arm properly, just yanked it round and round while gritting her teeth.

Now she's attempting to inject the needle through my

211

blanket. The needle is actually bending. I realize I don't need to fight back at all. I just let her believe she succeeded, and, to my amazement, she falls for it. After releasing the needle from my blankets, she leaves with the orderly, and I'm alone.

***

I've been here a full month. I'm told I can finally go home today. I believe no one. Last night I phoned Edward, stressing the need for him to show up at the hospital first thing in the morning. I've overheard the nurses, once again making frenzied plans to keep me longer. "Please, please get here early before they figure out another way to keep me here!" I pleaded with Edward.

Now it's the morning of what

I hope is my last day. I've packed all my belongings into plastic bags. I don't know how I managed to accumulate so much stuff! A nurse is looking through one of the bags. She pulls out some jeans with part of one leg cut off, a questioning look on her face.

"Oh." She says after some thought "I guess they had to cut off your clothes when you came in here." I don't know what to answer. I don't know why Ed brought me a bag of my material scraps that I use for making dolls. I pretend it all makes sense. I don't want to rock the boat, I need to go home.

Several nurses are looking through my other bags. They're discussing me as though I'm not even here. "We have to let her go home today." One of them tells the others in frustration "Nobody is going to believe she should be made to stay when she's actually packed all her bags and stuff!"

One of them asks if I brushed my teeth today. I lie and tell her I did. Now I'm concerned - my toothbrush is actually still in its package, unopened. "Did you have a shower this morning?" the nurse asks now. They're trying to trick me. I haven't showered or brushed my teeth the whole time I've been here. I wasn't able to get out of bed, and nobody mentioned it, so I forgot. Now I know they'll use this as their loophole to keep me, so I lie.

"Yes I brushed my teeth, and I had a bath." I tell the nurses. They glance at each other, there are no bath tubs here.

"Do you mean a sponge bath?" they ask? With relief, I tell them, yes.

I'm furtively attempting to insert my hand into the bag the nurses are looking through, to somehow open the package holding my toothbrush, so the nurses don't find it unopened, and realise I lied. One of them suddenly gives a shout, and pulls my hand out. I've cut my hand on the package. There's blood everywhere.

I pretend it's nothing. They'll use this to keep me, I know it. They're dashing around for gauze, barking at me to keep my hand elevated. Grabbing my arm and yanking it into the air whenever I forget and let it drop. Blood is pouring out because of the blood thinners I'm on. "It's nothing." I keep insisting "I'm sure it looks worse than it is." Please, please, I'm thinking, please don't make me stay.

My hand has been encased in a huge bandage. I can hear the staff at the front desk, talking about me, exclaiming "She acted like she didn't even care! There was blood everywhere and she couldn't care less!" They're arguing over keeping me longer. Suddenly 'Paris' comes running up the hall, very excited. The other nurses crowd around her. She has a new plan.

"I'm going to tell the doctors that Marian has been lying this whole time about her mother being dead." 'Paris' blurts out "I'm going to say 'I met Marian's mother in the cafeteria just the other day! She's alive and well! Marian is so crazy she made everything up. I could tell her mother wanted nothing to do with Marian because she's so crazy.' They'll have to keep Marian here

216

if they believe me that she lied about her mother."

The others are only slightly doubtful. "Maybe it will work." They say "It's worth a try." 'Paris' catches sight of one of the doctors, and scampers up to her to tell her the story. The doctor is unimpressed.

"I won't stop you." She tells 'Paris' "But I don't condone it. This is going too far. I want no part of it."

I'm crying on the phone again to Edward "Please come now! They've just about figured out a way to keep me here again!" One of the doctors passes my door. "Please let me leave today!" I cry to him "My mother really is dead, I didn't lie! My boyfriend is coming to pick me up. His name is Doug."

I don't know why I added that. And now it dawns on me that

I gave a wrong name. "His name isn't Doug, it's Edward!" I call out, realizing too late that I'm making myself sound crazier by the minute, and actually helping my enemies' case.

I hear the sock cutting doctor down the hall. I need to intercept him before the nurses fill him in on all that's gone on. But the nurses have descended on him now, everyone clamouring to be heard. "She didn't care that she was bleeding!" "She's been lying about her mother!" "She's too crazy to go home!"

He explodes. According to him, he's been trying to get rid of me all this time, and it's me who is fighting to stay.

"It's all lies!" I cry "None of that is true, I'm well enough to go home now!"

"I'm going back to my

office." Sighs the doctor. "But I'm going the long way – I don't want to go past her door!" They all chuckle sadly at his tired joke.

***

I've called Edward again, he's on his way. "They're trying to make me stay." I cried to him "It's important that you say your name is Doug. Also, please tell them my mother is dead. Please hurry."

Now I've taken up a post in my doorway, peering up the hall, anxious for Edward's arrival. I'm not allowed to leave the doorway of my room, because, they tell me, I'll bring my germs into the hall. Apparently I'm still contagious or something. Really it's just their method of keeping me from getting to Edward before they do, so they can convince him I'm too sick to go home.

"Nobody's coming to get you…" One of the nurses is mopping the hall floor and sings this news at me as she passes. She's enjoying my distress. "He's probably miles away by now. He's trying to get as far away from you as possible…." She's smiling slightly. And then I see him. Edward is coming up the hall toward me. He waves.

"Oh oh." The nurse mutters, hurrying to the cafeteria to discuss with 'Paris' this unexpected turn.

***

Edward and I are in my room, waiting for a doctor to talk with us. A counselor talked with me earlier, and preformed some memory tests on me. She told me I'll probably get dementia. "From the looks of

it, it's probably already started."
She said.

I've been discharged. I've
changed into my street clothes.
They're much too big now, except
for my sandals, which can only fit
over my swollen feet if I loosen
them all the way. One of the nurses
has combed my hair. She asked
shyly if she could wet it a little bit,
to make it stay off my face. She
was very motherly.

I hear the far off sound of the
nurses singing. Practicing for the
reality show. I mention it to
Edward, but it makes him
impatient. "There's no singing."
He tells me firmly. "Nobody is
singing." But I hear it clearly,
they're singing one of my poems. I
begin to say this, then stop. No
more crazy, I need to get out of
here. I pretend to agree that no one
is singing.

UPDATE

At this writing, it's been 5 ½ years since I was diagnosed with liver cirrhosis, and spent a month in the hospital. I had my last drink that morning. I've been sober for 5 ½ years.

Cirrhosis makes you susceptible to cancer, and my latest ultrasound showed two spots on my liver. During the nine months I had to wait, to find out if it was cancer, I had a colonoscopy, gastroscopy, and CT scan. Two days ago, my sister and I went to my specialist to discuss the results.

I had only been a believer in Christ for a few months when I found out I might have cancer. God caught me just in time, so that I would have Him to lean on. For the nine months that I've waited to find out if the spots are cancerous, I have NOT been afraid. My relationship with God has flourished! And as I look back, I can see clearly that He had everything arranged perfectly, just so I would be safe and supported during this experience.

Liver Cirrhosis has been a huge blessing for me. Because of it, I was forced to stop drinking. It also played a part in bringing me back to my home-city, my family, and most importantly, God. If this intersession hadn't happened I would be drunk right now, or dead.

Finding out I might have cancer became an even bigger blessing, because it happened right after I accepted Christ, so this added a whole other dimension to the experience. Having my faith tested like this so soon after becoming a believer was an exhilarating experience! I fell in love, completely, with God. These past nine months have been a celebration of Joy that comes from God alone, and has nothing whatever to do with one's circumstances.

I was fully prepared to hear that I had cancer. I had some butterflies in my stomach as the doctor sat down, and I felt the beginning of tears, but they would have been tears of sadness, not fear. And they never came, because the doctor told me what I never expected to hear.

First she told me I don't have cancer. Then she told me that some of the damage from the cirrhosis has been healed – I had varicose veins in my stomach, because the arteries to my liver shut down and the blood had to be rerouted through my stomach, putting strain on those arteries. During my last visit we had talked about the possibility of putting bands around them to prevent bursting. Now they are completely healed. I saw the pictures.

Then she told me 'there is nothing to suggest that you still have liver cirrhosis'. I was not misdiagnosed. I have test results going back through these past five years, showing the damage, and symptoms that were worsening. I had liver cirrhosis, and now I don't. God healed me.

Without making any claims to anything, here is a list of 'Gods Medicine Food' that I've been eating. I personally believe that God used this food as a way to heal me.

- Homemade kombucha (fermented tea, flavoured with berries, fruits, raw ginger, spices …). I have several glasses every day. It's a probiotic, and has naturally detoxifying properties like gluconic acid that targets the liver.

- Homemade ditche malch - Thick milk, made by leaving goat's milk in a nylon covered jar under my dining table for a few days until it thickens, then dividing it among two jars, topping up with more goat's milk, and repeating this with more jars, until it thickens within 24 hours. By now I have about six jars full. Then I pour into milk bottles, cover with lids, and store them in the fridge. I pour this over oatmeal. It's a great probiotic.

- Homemade kefir - I make it with my goat ditche malch, and ferment it twice. The first time with the kefir grains, the second time I strain them out, then add dates, fruit slices, or berries for a second ferment. This way it's twice as probiotic. It also boosts immunity and helps prevent cancer. I have a glass of this before supper every day.

- Homemade sauerkraut - From one cabbage I get 6-7 jars. I add shredded carrots to a couple, and garlic to others, anything I can think of, some I leave plain. It is an immune system booster, a probiotic and it provides fiber for my compromised digestive system. I eat one baseball sized portion every day.

- Lemon dessert – A cancer preventative made with four whole lemons, ½ cup extra virgin olive oil, ½ cup raw honey, all mixed in the blender until smooth. I take one tablespoon every day.

- Yerba Mate – A tea, very much enjoyed in South America. It's full of vitamins, fibers, and antioxidants. I drink at least 6 -7 horn-fulls (you drink it from a horn, isn't that great?!) every day, sometimes more. I take it with honey.

- Nuts and seeds – A great source of fiber, and healthy

fats. Walnuts are also healing for brain damage, which I have. I keep small bowls of walnuts, cashews, almonds, sunflower seeds, etc. on a tray, and eat handfuls of these together with honey soaked ginger while I'm drinking matte. I also add these nuts and seeds to every meal I can. I always sprout (soak for at least 8 hours, usually overnight), then dehydrate them for a couple of hours. I also skin the almonds before dehydrating them. This makes them all easier to digest.

- Honey soaked ginger –
  Ginger is a blood thinner, and aid for nausea. It also reduces pain and inflammation. Honey is full of antioxidants,

vitamins, and minerals. I peel and chop a large piece of ginger into bite sized pieces, giving me about 1½ - 2 cups. Simmer the ginger in ½ cup raw honey, and ½ cup water, uncovered, for ½ hour, then covered for ½ hour. Sieve the ginger out, and use the remaining ginger/honey water for syrup or salad dressing, or, my latest discovery – drizzled over popcorn.

- Juicing – Provides vitamins, minerals, antioxidants. It cleanses the liver, and is easily digested – especially good for a compromised digestive system. I put in any and all veggies, fruits and greens that I can think of, and add a ½ pinkie sized piece of turmeric, and the same amount of fresh ginger. I have one glass of juice every morning on an empty stomach.

- Smoothies – Provides nutrients, antioxidants … each smoothie is different, and depends on what I have available. Each fruit and veggie I put in has its own unique store of gifts for my health. I also add chia, and flax seeds, and psyllium husks. To thin it I add either homemade kombucha, diche malch, goat's milk, or whey. I have one glass every day.

- Whey – Provides vitamins, minerals, electrolytes, excellent for gut health. I make it by leaving a jar of ditche malch under the table for a week or so longer than usual. When it becomes quite thickened, I sieve it, saving the solid part (the curds) to use as sour cream, or sometimes it turns into what I believe is cottage cheese! I blend it with honey, or garlic, and use it as a dip. The liquid is called whey. I keep both the curds, and the whey in the fridge.

I've found that just by substituting my typical heavy German meals with things like sweet potatoes, sauerkraut, squash, chicken, turkey or fish, etc., and sauces made from blenderised veggies and/or fruit, herbs and spices, I feel satisfied, rather than unpleasantly full.

I have to include my favourite breakfast:

- ½ bowl cooked porridge oats (ancient grain blend), topped with …
- At least 1 cup of berries and fruit
- Handful of raisins and chopped dates
- Handful of soaked & dehydrated, chopped nuts and seeds
- 1 T hemp hearts
- 1 tsp. psyllium husks
- 1 tsp. ea. ground chia and flax seeds
- Ditche malch poured over everything

WHAT I STOPPED EATING
(although I do believe in cheating once in a while if done responsibly)

- I stopped eating processed food, sticking to fresh, or if necessary, frozen fruits, veggies and greens.
- I stopped eating fast food
- I cut way down on fried food, and use coconut oil when I do fry my food
- I stopped eating red meat
- I stopped eating junk food
- I practically stopped eating bread
- I stopped eating store bought sauces and spreads except for a select few good ones that I am in the process of replacing with homemade recipes
- I stopped eating sugar
- I cut way back on cheese, and

learned to make my own nut cheese!

- I stopped drinking cow's milk, and all other milks except goat's milk
- I stopped drinking alcohol, and taking painkillers (Percodan, oxy's, and codeine)

I believe that changing my diet to God's Medicine Food (and, of course, no longer drinking) healed me of liver cirrhosis. I believe that God made this happen. I know for sure that my relationship with God is the biggest, most important part of the medicine that healed me. I gave all my worries to Him, and concentrated on laughing and enjoying life.

During the first 4 ½ years that I was sick, I did not know God. I didn't know that I had this great comforter and friend to help me. But once I became a believer, all of that changed. My life is full of blessings. And Jesus is my best friend. I can live my life now, knowing that I am not afraid to die, because I'm right with God. What a great gift.

*Other books by Marian Toews:

'The Heavens Declare the Glory of God' (My testimony, and a 10 day devotional) **'He Heals the Broken Hearted and Binds Up their Wounds'** (A 10 day devotional) **'Noah's Ark'** (A children's illustrated bible story)

Made in the USA
Middletown, DE
28 January 2017